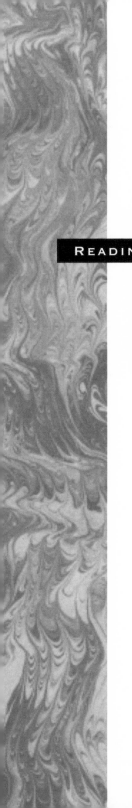

READINGS ON

EMILY DICKINSON

OTHER TITLES IN THE GREENHAVEN PRESS
LITERARY COMPANION SERIES:

AMERICAN AUTHORS

Maya Angelou
Nathaniel Hawthorne
Ernest Hemingway
Herman Melville
Arthur Miller
John Steinbeck
Mark Twain

BRITISH AUTHORS

Jane Austen

WORLD AUTHORS

Sophocles

BRITISH LITERATURE

The Canterbury Tales
Lord of the Flies
Shakespeare: The Comedies
Shakespeare: The Sonnets
Shakespeare: The Tragedies
A Tale of Two Cities

THE GREENHAVEN PRESS
Literary Companion
TO AMERICAN AUTHORS

READINGS ON

EMILY DICKINSON

David Bender, *Publisher*
Bruno Leone, *Executive Editor*
Scott Barbour, *Managing Editor*
Bonnie Szumski, *Series Editor*
Tamara Johnson, *Book Editor*

Greenhaven Press, San Diego, CA

Library of Congress Cataloging-in-Publication Data

Readings on Emily Dickinson / Tamara Johnson, book editor.
        p.   cm. — (The Greenhaven Press literary com-
    panion to American authors)
    Includes bibliographical references and index.
    ISBN 1-56510-634-2 (pbk. : alk. paper). —
ISBN 1-56510-635-0 (lib. : alk. paper)
    1. Dickinson, Emily, 1830–1886—Criticism and
interpretation. 2. Women and literature—Massachusetts
—History—19th century. I. Johnson, Tamara. II. Series.
PS1541.Z5R43   1997
811'.4—dc20   96-44979
                                                         CIP

Cover photo: Amherst College Library

Copyright ©1997 by Greenhaven Press, Inc.
PO Box 289009
San Diego, CA 92198-9009
Printed in the U.S.A.

When much in the Woods as a little Girl, I was told that the snake would bite me, that I might pick a poisonous flower, or Goblins kidnap me, but I went along and met no one but Angels, who were far shyer of me than I could be of them, so I haven't that confidence in fraud in which many exercise.

Emily Dickinson

Contents

Chapter 1: Emily Dickinson: The Woman and the Poet

Chapter 2: Poetic Analysis

Chapter 3: Dickinson's Poetic Themes

FOREWORD

> *"'Tis the good reader that*
> *makes the good book."*
>
> Ralph Waldo Emerson

The story's bare facts are simple: The captain, an old and scarred seafarer, walks with a peg leg made of whale ivory. He relentlessly drives his crew to hunt the world's oceans for the great white whale that crippled him. After a long search, the ship encounters the whale and a fierce battle ensues. Finally the captain drives his harpoon into the whale, but the harpoon line catches the captain about the neck and drags him to his death.

A simple story, a straightforward plot—yet, since the 1851 publication of Herman Melville's *Moby-Dick*, readers and critics have found many meanings in the struggle between Captain Ahab and the whale. To some, the novel is a cautionary tale that depicts how Ahab's obsession with revenge leads to his insanity and death. Others believe that the whale represents the unknowable secrets of the universe and that Ahab is a tragic hero who dares to challenge fate by attempting to discover this knowledge. Perhaps Melville intended Ahab as a criticism of Americans' tendency to become involved in well-intentioned but irrational causes. Or did Melville model Ahab after himself, letting his fictional character express his anger at what he perceived as a cruel and distant god?

Although literary critics disagree over the meaning of *Moby-Dick*, readers do not need to choose one particular interpretation in order to gain an understanding of Melville's novel. Instead, by examining various analyses, they can gain numerous insights into the issues that lie under the surface of the basic plot. Studying the writings of literary critics can also aid readers in making their own assessments of *Moby-Dick* and other literary works and in developing analytical thinking skills.

The Greenhaven Literary Companion Series was created with these goals in mind. Designed for young adults, this unique anthology series provides an engaging and comprehensive introduction to literary analysis and criticism. The essays included in the Literary Companion Series are chosen for their accessibility to a young adult audience and are expertly edited in consideration of both the reading and comprehension levels of this audience. In addition, each essay is introduced by a concise summation that presents the contributing writer's main themes and insights. Every anthology in the Literary Companion Series contains a varied selection of critical essays that cover a wide time span and express diverse views. Wherever possible, primary sources are represented through excerpts from authors' notebooks, letters, and journals and through contemporary criticism.

Each title in the Literary Companion Series pays careful consideration to the historical context of the particular author or literary work. In-depth biographies and detailed chronologies reveal important aspects of authors' lives and emphasize the historical events and social milieu that influenced their writings. To facilitate further research, every anthology includes primary and secondary source bibliographies of articles and/or books selected for their suitability for young adults. These engaging features make the Greenhaven Literary Companion series ideal for introducing students to literary analysis in the classroom or as a library resource for young adults researching the world's great authors and literature.

Exceptional in its focus on young adults, the Greenhaven Literary Companion Series strives to present literary criticism in a compelling and accessible format. Every title in the series is intended to spark readers' interest in leading American and world authors, to help them broaden their understanding of literature, and to encourage them to formulate their own analyses of the literary works that they read. It is the editors' hope that young adult readers will find these anthologies to be true companions in their study of literature.

INTRODUCTION

Much beloved throughout the world, Emily Dickinson was the first American poet to successfully bridge the gap between nineteenth-century lyric verse—in the tradition of Edgar Allan Poe, Herman Melville, and Ralph Waldo Emerson—and the modern free verse championed by Walt Whitman. Unlike Whitman, who simply discarded popular assumptions about rhyme, meter, and rhythm in order to pursue his own rambling muse, Dickinson pushed the limits of traditional form. In her quiet reflections on home and nature, rhyme is stretched to its furthest capabilities, with jarring results. Her meditations on death, desire, and spiritual confusion are delicate yet bold in their honesty. More than a hundred years after her death her poetry continues to influence the way readers look at literature.

A number of the essays included in the Greenhaven Literary Companion to Emily Dickinson are written by poets. Occasionally the essays are accompanied by poetic tributes to Dickinson, who continues to inspire poets and critics alike. As a whole, the writers and scholars represented in this collection provide teachers and students with a range of opinion on Dickinson—who has not always been well received. The varied viewpoints reflect alternative methods scholars use for better understanding a work of poetry, including cultural, historical, and biographical analyses. These varied approaches allow students to discover diverse materials from which to generate topics for research papers, group studies, and oral presentations.

The essays in this companion are selected and organized for students encountering Emily Dickinson for the first time. Collectively they demonstrate a range of possibilities for the beginning scholar. Some essays offer insight into the poet's life and its influence on her work. Some select specific poems for line-by-line analysis. Others evaluate Dickinson's body of work and rank her among other poets. The essays serve not only as models but represent the large numbers of studies that continue to be published. Additional listings at the end of this book point students toward various publications that are recommended for further research.

The brief biography is designed to provide students with a basic sketch of Dickinson's life: when and where she was born, the cultural climate and educational opportunities of her time, some difficulties she encountered in writing and publishing her poetry, and the events that led to the posthumous discovery of her work. Because details of Dickinson's life are sketchy, several excerpts from letters by people who knew the poet are included. Although Dickinson's poetry does have some autobiographical elements, care has been taken not to confuse the speaker of the poems with Emily Dickinson herself.

This collection has several important features. Most of the essays concern a single, focused topic, either a single idea or a unique approach to a particular work. Introductions clarify and summarize the main point so that the reader will know what to expect. Interspersed within the essays, the reader will find inserts that add authenticity, supplementary information, or illustrative anecdotes. Inserts are drawn from sources such as original letters by Dickinson and poems by the authors. *Readings on Emily Dickinson* gives students a wide selection of critical essays to explore a unique and complex poet.

EMILY DICKINSON: A BIOGRAPHY

Emily Dickinson lived and died in the small Massachusetts farming village of Amherst. Her New England ancestors had endured tough times in the town, stressing the values of hard work, religious fervor, and frugality. Among her Puritan fore-fathers, even words were chosen carefully so as not to waste them, a trait that Emily seems to have instinctively incorpo-rated in her highly unusual poems. With the exception of a year at Mount Holyoke Seminary for Girls, a nearby boarding school, and several short trips to Boston, Washington, and Philadelphia, Emily always lived under the same roof as her parents and sister, Lavinia. Even after marrying, her brother, Austin, moved just next door, where the three siblings could continue to spend many hours together in conversation.

An intensely private woman, Emily grew to avoid contact with all but her immediate family. She ordered her personal letters burned upon her death. Her poetry, which Lavinia found in bundles inside her desk, survives today only be-cause her sister did not see fit to burn it. Not all the poems were saved, however. Some were destroyed with the letters. Others were altered so as not to reveal too much about the life of the woman many knew only as the "Myth of Amherst."

THE IMPORTANCE OF HOME AND FAMILY

Emily Dickinson's childhood seems relatively uneventful. She was born on December 10, 1830, the middle child of Ed-ward Dickinson and Emily Norcross, two of Amherst's most respected citizens. Edward was a lawyer, a politician, and the treasurer of Amherst College. Emily's father placed a high value on education, writing often while on business trips to remind his children to study. Emily Norcross, daugh-ter of a prosperous family, saw her marriage to Edward as a practical decision rather than the result of a romantic courtship. Edward looked upon his engagement to Miss Norcross rather dispassionately as well, having found, as he wrote shortly before the marriage, a woman with whom he could live out his vision of the perfect married couple:

> May we be virtuous, intelligent, industrious and by the exercise of every virtue, & the cultivation of every excellence, be esteemed and respected & beloved by all—We must be determined to do our duty to each other, & to all our friends, and let others do as they may.

To the Dickinsons, the Homestead, as they called their large brick house, was "the real world." The day began with Edward Dickinson's deep voice reading from the Bible or, when Mr. Dickinson was on one of his frequent business trips, in quiet study and contemplation. Though the Dickinsons had servants, nineteenth-century domestic duties were a big part of Emily's day as well. Mrs. Dickinson taught her daughters to bake bread, wash clothes, sew, and clean house, jobs Emily often complained about in letters to friends and relatives. Lavinia (or Vinnie as Emily's sister was called), seems to have found household tasks more agreeable than Emily did.

It is clear that despite their many chores, both girls loved the Homestead. Their letters reveal homesickness not only when they were away from home themselves, but also when a family member was missing from the household. When Austin was away at law school, for example, Emily wrote to him at Harvard in October 1851:

> You had a windy evening going back to Boston, and we thought of you many times and hoped you would not be cold. Our fire burned so cheerfully I couldn't help thinking of how many were *here* and how many were *away*, and I wished so many times during that long evening that the door would open and you come walking in. Home is holy—nothing of doubt or distrust can enter its blessed portals. I feel it more and more as the great world goes on and one another forsake, in whom you place your trust—here seems indeed to be a bit of Eden.

Though all the siblings were close, the bond between Austin and Emily was special. Outwardly shy, Emily enjoyed her brother's irreverent humor and they both shared a deep appreciation for nature. When Austin married, it was to Susan Gilbert, one of Emily's closest friends. Susan shared Emily's sharp wit and love of poetry, an interest Austin had developed as well. On at least one occasion, Austin asked Emily for her opinion of some poems he had written. Though he clearly respected Emily's judgment, he had no idea what brilliance Emily possessed. Nor did Susan, who received close to a hundred poems from Emily throughout her life.

EDUCATION AND A SOCIAL LIFE

Though Emily was known throughout Amherst as a poet, the extent of her talent was hidden from nearly everyone. As a child, she was never singled out by teachers as particularly gifted. In fact, her school years seem oddly unremarkable. She studied such subjects as mathematics, geography, ancient history, and English grammar. After a year at Mount Holyoke in 1847, Emily dropped out, citing illness. Though she did in fact miss some school due to a bad cough, it seems unlikely that this was reason enough for her to return home.

She was often homesick; a longing for her family and for Amherst weighed heavily on her mind. It is possible that the curriculum at Mount Holyoke did not provide the intellectual challenge that she had expected. Emily was a voracious reader, and there was always a variety of books and newspapers at the Homestead. Though her father frowned on certain reading materials, afraid they would "joggle the mind," Emily was still able to read from a wide spectrum of books including Shakespeare and her contemporaries George Eliot and Charlotte and Emily Brontë.

Of course, the Bible was a constant and powerful influence, as well. By the time Emily entered her teens, religious revivals were taking place all over New England. Revivals, gatherings led by itinerant charismatic preachers, or circuit riders, were often attended by crowds so large no building could hold them. There was tremendous pressure at such meetings for spectators to commit to Christianity or to a specific Christian congregation, and in the excitement of the moment many did.

Similar pressure was in evidence at Mount Holyoke, where students were openly encouraged to publicly declare their devotion to Christ. Emily, though deeply interested in spiritual matters, was afraid of being "easily deceived," and when the girls were asked one by one to declare their faith Emily was unable to do so. This perceived failing distressed her deeply, as she wanted to count herself among the converted as her roommate and cousin Emily Lavinia Norcross did. Long discussions on this subject with her friend Abiah Root continued by letter for many years. The continued pressure on Emily to declare what she could not feel in her heart probably played a role in Emily's decision to leave Mount Holyoke. Certainly the question of faith became a constant theme in her poetry.

Back in Amherst, Emily resumed the interests of a normal teenager. There were lots of parties to attend, as well as taffy pulls and carriage rides. Social calls were common etiquette and both Vinnie and Emily either went calling or received visitors almost every day. Some of the visitors were young lawyers from Mr. Dickinson's law office. Others were university students. Exchanging valentines was a popular custom: Emily wrote a Valentine's Day poem, possibly to a young man named George Howland, that was printed in the *Springfield Republican* in 1852.

Emily Dickinson did not start writing poetry seriously, however, until about 1858, when she was in her late twenties. She was admired by then for her piano playing, her singing voice, and her sense of humor. She was considered well liked and attractive if not beautiful. Suddenly, she withdrew from nearly all social activity and began writing furiously. She stashed poems in her sewing basket, wrote ideas on the back of grocery lists. Some poems she recopied carefully, then bound with thread and hid in her dresser drawers.

People began to call her "the myth" because she was so rarely seen in public. Rumors began to circulate about her delicate mind, and there was speculation that she had fallen in love and had been rejected, possibly by a married man. While it is unclear whether a single event or circumstance was responsible for such a sudden and irrepressible flash of inspiration coupled with reclusiveness, several events no doubt had tremendous impact on Emily's life.

AUSTIN'S MARRIAGE

One event that certainly affected Emily deeply was her brother's marriage to Susan. Emily and Susan were such close friends that several biographers have concluded that it was Emily rather than Austin who was in love with Susan. Certainly the elder Mr. Dickinson was charmed early on by the bright and energetic girl his son was courting, often escorting Susan home after her visits to the Homestead. In anticipation of Austin's marriage, Edward built the couple a home next to his own. It was hoped that the Evergreens, as they called the new house, would represent a new generation of Dickinsons. With father and son now legal partners as well, the prestige of the Dickinson name could only have been seen as a move up for Susan, a barkeeper's daughter whose childhood was marred by her father's alcoholism.

Austin and Sue's marriage was not a happy one. Though at first he kept his unhappiness from the family—perhaps he was afraid to disappoint Edward—Austin would later describe his July 1856 wedding as "going to his execution." Sue's high-spirited nature began to take on a cruel edge and what she said in anger Austin would beg her to take back. When two orphaned cousins, Anna and Clara Newman, came to live at the Evergreens in 1858, Sue, according to family friends, enjoyed treating them like poor relations. Visitors to the Evergreens observed "chaotic behavior" and "bursts of temper." Even before the wedding, letters from Emily to Sue point to some sort of falling out between the women:

> Sue—you can go or stay—There is but one alternative—We differ often lately and this must be the last.

> You need not fear to leave me lest I should be alone, for I often part with things I fancy I have loved,—sometimes to the grave and sometimes to an oblivion rather bitterer than death— thus my heart bleeds so frequently I shant mind the hemorrhage, and I only add an agony to previous ones.

The sisters-in-law made up, however, and for two years after the wedding Emily spent a lot of time at the Evergreens. Because of Austin's prestige in the community and, following his father, his position as treasurer of Amherst College, guests at the Evergreens often included prominent intellectuals. Sue's preference for a more bohemian crowd brought artists and professionals together, a mix Emily enjoyed. Her father apparently did not: On one occasion Edward Dickinson, thinking it indecent for Emily to be out so late, showed up at midnight to escort his daughter home from the Evergreens, an incident that was surely embarrassing for her.

As Austin became less and less comfortable opening his house to the odd array of characters his wife attracted, he began taking solitary night walks while his houseguests carried on in what he referred to as "my wife's tavern." Occasionally his oldest sister would accompany him. Emily too was tiring of the merrymaking. When the Austin Dickinsons entertained celebrated poet and philosopher Ralph Waldo Emerson in December of 1857, Emily did not attend the gathering. Whether another rift had occurred is unclear, but, in any case, as the atmosphere at the Evergreens became ever more erratic, life at the Homestead assumed its opposite character. Austin began to see the Homestead as a haven from Susan, whose temper had become so explosive she had taken to throwing knives.

Austin's despair in his relationship with Susan culminated in an affair with Mabel Loomis Todd, beginning in 1882. Todd was a family friend and frequent visitor at the Evergreens; tensions between Susan and Austin thereafter were at times nearly unbearable.

Susan felt, perhaps correctly, that the Dickinson sisters sided with their brother in his decision to openly pursue his romance with Mabel (who was also married, to David Peck Todd, a professor of astronomy at Amherst College and a friend of Austin's in spite of the affair). The atmosphere between the Evergreens and the Homestead turned from icy to outwardly hostile. Susan's acid tongue wounded Emily so deeply at times that Vinnie claimed Susan's meanness shortened Emily's life by ten years. At the least, the close relationship between Sue and Emily dissolved.

MRS. DICKINSON'S CONVALESCENCE

While the hostility between the Evergreens and the Homestead was hard on Emily, another situation predating the feud with Susan was not only emotionally taxing for Emily, but physically exhausting as well. When Mrs. Dickinson fell ill with an undiagnosed malady (some suspect hypochondria) in November 1855, responsibility for her care fell to her daughters. Though Mrs. Dickinson survived her husband by eight years, she was bedridden much of her later life and needed constant attention until her death in November 1882.

Emily, who was not particularly close to her mother, felt this nearly thirty-year burden acutely. Clearly the most brilliant of the Dickinson children, she was offered no financial or emotional encouragement to pursue her intellectual or literary interests as was the Harvard-educated Austin. Though in childhood the Dickinson girls were schooled in nearly the same manner as their brother, and though in theory Edward Dickinson wanted his girls to receive a well-rounded education, Edward Dickinson did not like his grown daughters to appear too literary. In an essay he wrote for the *New England Inquirer* in 1827, Emily's father had this to say about women's role in society:

> What duties were females designed to perform? Were they intended for Rulers, or Legislators, or Soldiers? Were they intended for the learned professions;—to engage in those branches of business, which require the exertion of great strength, or the exercise of great skill?...
>
> Modesty and sweetness of disposition, and patience and forbearance and fortitude, are the cardinal virtues of the female sex.... These will atone for the want of brilliant talents, or great attainment.

With her mother's illness, Emily, who had always known there was more to life than drudgery, and who had always hurried through her housework, her sewing, and her cleaning in order to take long walks in the garden with her dog Carlo, now had additional demands on her free time. Increasingly, she viewed such interests as fashion as time-consuming and trivial distractions, and as she looked for ways to simplify her life, she adopted a wardrobe made up almost entirely of white dresses, which did not have to be matched or color coordinated and which required no special laundering beyond the bleaching already given to the sheets and towels.

This costume added an air of mystery to the woman who now rarely left her house. With no interest in Susan's gatherings, and with the shopping and visiting left to the more sociable Vinnie, Emily's contact with the outside world was conducted primarily through the mail. Nevertheless, the letters she wrote to friends and neighbors were extraordinary, often taking on the cadence of poetry themselves.

A TIME OF MANY PARTINGS

As childhood friends married and began to leave Amherst with their husbands, Emily and Vinnie shared the additional isolation of being labeled spinsters in the community. By 1858, the most eligible of Amherst's citizens had stopped thinking of Emily as a suitable wife. Abiah Root and other girlfriends Emily had once held in close confidence wrote rarely once they were married.

In addition, as many as thirty-three young acquaintances of Emily's died between 1851 and 1854, including Emily Lavinia Norcross, with whom Emily had stayed in close contact since Mount Holyoke. These losses deeply affected

Emily, whose poetry almost obsessively focuses on death. In November 1858 she wrote to some family friends, Dr. and Mrs. Josiah Gilbert:

> I can't stay any longer in a world of death. Austin is ill of scarlet fever. I buried my garden last week—our man Dick, lost a little girl through the scarlet fever. I thought perhaps that *you* were dead, and not knowing the sexton's address, interrogated the daisies. Ah! dainty—dainty Death! Ah! democratic Death! Grasping the proudest zinnia from my purple garden.

ONLY SEVEN POEMS PUBLISHED

Despite the numerous losses and disappointments Emily suffered, a theme of hope persisted in her poetry and in her life. Frustrated in her few attempts to seek guidance from other writers, she continued writing even more seriously in isolation, but with a determination that must have come from a deep inner confidence in her own abilities.

After answering a call for submissions in the *Atlantic Monthly* in 1862, for example, Emily received a polite reply from Colonel Thomas Wentworth Higginson, a distinguished man of letters who was serving as editor for the magazine's younger writers. Higginson did not submit Emily's work for publication, and even wrote to the *Atlantic* senior editor, James T. Fields, the day after receiving Emily's poems: "I foresee that 'Young Contributor' will send me worse things than ever now. Two such specimens came yesterday & day before—fortunately *not* to be forwarded for publication!" Still, Emily continued to seek Higginson's advice, sending him numerous poems during a twenty-year correspondence. Not until long after her death was Higginson forced to recognize his student's genius.

Two writers who had more confidence in Emily's writing were Helen Hunt Jackson, a poet and novelist who had herself grown up in Amherst and who urged Emily to send her poetry out for publication, and Mabel Loomis Todd, who was instrumental in getting the poems published after Emily's death. Emily was successful in publishing only seven of her poems during her lifetime. All of the poems were published anonymously and were so edited that Emily was hesitant to entrust further work to the whims of editors who clearly misunderstood it.

When widespread publication of her work began to seem less and less likely, Emily began to bind her poems into several homemade books, or fascicles. In 1864 her writing was interrupted when she was forced to travel to Boston for eye treatment. She remained there for seven months and on her return had difficulty resuming her regular chores and, presumably, her writing.

When her father died suddenly in 1874, Emily's grief was deep. She continued to write, although not with the frequency of previous years, and her isolation became so deep that she refused to meet visitors face to face, preferring to talk to them from behind a screen or door. Eventually she watered her garden in the dark so as not to be seen. Yet, she continued her many correspondences, writing draft after draft of her letters before sending them out. Often she would include a poem, which a few friends might circulate among themselves. Many of Amherst's citizens were curious to meet her. One eager for the opportunity was Mabel Loomis Todd, who wrote in her journal:

> [Austin's] sister Emily is called in Amherst "the myth." She has not been out of her house for fifteen years. One inevitably thinks of [Dickens's eccentric] Miss Havisham in speaking of her. She writes the strangest poems, & very remarkable ones. She is in many respects a genius. She wears always white, & has her hair arranged as was the fashion fifteen years ago when she went into retirement. She wanted me to come and sing to her, but she would not see me. She has frequently sent me flowers and poems, & we have a very pleasant friendship in that way. So last Sunday I went over there with Mr. Dickinson. . . . It was odd to think, as my voice rang out through the big silent house that Miss Emily in her weird white dress was outside in the shadow hearing every word, & the mother, bed-ridden for years was listening up the stairs. When I stopped Emily sent me in a glass of rich sherry & a poem written as I sang. I know I shall yet see her. No one has seen her in all those years except her own family. She is very brilliant and strong, but has become disgusted with society & declared she would leave it when she was quite young.

Mabel never did see Emily, who died of a kidney disease in 1886. But she did get to read the over eighteen hundred poems or fragments of poems hidden among her belongings, and she was ultimately responsible for their publication.

A SISTER'S PERSISTENCE LEADS TO RECOGNITION

Vinnie was the one who found the poems and, immediately recognizing their quality, who was determined to have Emily's talent acknowledged. Though she and Susan were still barely speaking, she knew of her sister-in-law's interest in poetry and asked if Susan would edit a few of the poems for her. Seeing neither public interest nor profit in Emily's work, Susan refused. Vinnie then turned to Mabel, who was well liked in Amherst and well connected in literary circles. Mabel agreed not only to edit Emily's poetry, but to try to persuade Colonel Higginson to change his opinion of its worth.

Higginson advised against a book, finding the poems "too crude in form," but Mabel persisted, sending her select favorites until he finally admitted there were many that were "passable." When he insisted on giving the poems titles, however, they were occasionally so lacking in a basic understanding of the poems that Mabel had to intervene. But Higginson's approval was crucial. Even with it, Mabel had a difficult time finding a publisher to accept the poems. After several rejections, Vinnie offered to pay for the initial costs, afraid that with any further delays in publication, Emily's friends and acquaintances would grow old and die, leaving no one to appreciate her poems.

She need not have worried. *Poems*, published in 1890, created such a stir that a second series of Emily's poetry was released in 1891, followed by *Letters* in 1894 and a third series of *Poems* in 1896. Sales were so high there was a court battle over the royalties, ending with Vinnie awarded copyright ownership. In 1914, Susan and Austin's daughter Mattie (Martha Dickinson Bianchi) edited two more books: *The Life and Letters of Emily Dickinson* and *The Complete Poems of Emily Dickinson.*

Despite enormous public interest, some early critics responded unfavorably to Dickinson's poems because she did not adhere to the strict conventions of rhyme and meter of the day. Unlike her contemporary Walt Whitman, who did away with rhyme and meter altogether, Dickinson stretched the limits of traditional form by making use of near or slant rhymes, using the dash for emphasis, and employing capitalization for effect. Her innovations preceded those of some experimental or postmodern poets by as much as one hundred years.

Like her rhymes, the messages of her poems are often just within the reach of understanding. "Tell all the Truth but tell it slant," begins one, showing that the heart of understanding is usually not in what seems most obvious to us, but in what lies just under the surface. Like riddles, her definitions of such concepts as love, faith, and honesty stretch our mental faculties so that the reader begins to question definitions once taken for granted. Then, just as knowledge gets most slippery, Dickinson gives the reader a concrete image to hold on to:

> This World is not Conclusion.
> A Species stands beyond—
> Invisible, as Music—
> But positive, as Sound—
> It beckons, and it baffles—
> Philosophy—don't know—
> And through a Riddle, at the last—
> Sagacity, must go—
> To guess it, puzzles scholars—
> To gain it, Men have borne
> Contempt of Generations
> And Crucifixion, shown—
> Faith slips—and laughs, and rallies—
> Blushes, if any see—
> Plucks at a Twig of Evidence—
> And asks a Vane, the way—
> Much Gesture, from the Pulpit—
> Strong Hallelujahs roll—
> Narcotics cannot still the Tooth
> That nibbles at the soul—
>   (501)

Each poem on hope, or nature, or God, shows that there is not a single all-encompassing truth, but many delicate truths that change from person to person, day to day, poem to poem.

Today, Dickinson's place in American poetry is secure. Poets such as Hart Crane, Adrienne Rich, and Amy Lowell have expressed their gratitude for Dickinson's work in their own poetry. Her poems have been read all over the world and have been translated into many languages. In examining the essays contained in this volume, readers may gain a deeper appreciation of Emily Dickinson's work.

CHAPTER 1

Emily Dickinson: The Woman and the Poet

Dickinson Constructed Her Own Elusive Image

Joyce Carol Oates

A prolific fiction writer and respected literary critic, Joyce Carol Oates won the National Book Award in 1970 for her novel *them*. The following excerpt is from a 1986 lecture in which Oates states that "writing is invariably an act of rebellion" and suggests that the question of Dickinson's true identity remains unanswerable at least in part because the persona, or poetic identity, Dickinson created is difficult to distinguish from her true inner nature—a nature that even the poet herself described largely through contradiction.

Emily Dickinson is the most paradoxical of poets: the very poet of paradox. By way of voluminous biographical material, not to mention the extraordinary intimacy of her poetry, it would seem that we know everything about her: yet the common experience of reading her work, particularly if the poems are read sequentially, is that we come away seeming to know nothing. We would recognize her inimitable voice anywhere—in the "prose" of her letters no less than in her poetry—yet it is a voice of the most deliberate, the most teasing anonymity. "I'm Nobody!" is a proclamation to be interpreted in the most literal of ways. Like no other poet before her and like very few after her—Rilke comes most readily to mind, and, perhaps, Yeats and Lawrence—Dickinson exposes her heart's most subtle secrets; she confesses the very sentiments that, in society, would have embarrassed her dog (to paraphrase a remark of Dickinson's to Thomas Wentworth Higginson, explaining her aversion for the company of most people, whose prattle of "Hallowed things" offended her). Yet who is this "I" at the center of experience? In her astonishing body of 1,775 poems Dickinson records what is

From Joyce Carol Oates, "'Soul at the White Heat': The Romance of Emily Dickinson's Poetry," in *(Woman) Writer: Occasions and Opportunities* (New York: Dutton, 1988). Copyright The Ontario Review, Inc. Reprinted by permission of the author.

surely one of the most meticulous examinations of the phe-
nomenon of human "consciousness" ever undertaken. The
poet's persona—the tantalizing "I"—seems, in nearly every
poem, to be addressing us directly with perceptions that are
ours as well as hers. (Or his: these "Representatives of the
Verse," though speaking in Dickinson's voice, are not re-
stricted to the female gender.) The poems' refusal to be
rhetorical, their daunting intimacy, suggests the self-evident
in the way that certain Zen koans and riddles suggest the
self-evident while being indecipherable. But what is chal-
lenged is, perhaps, "meaning" itself:

> Wonder—is not precisely Knowing
> And not precisely Knowing not—
> A beautiful but bleak condition
> He has not lived who has not felt—
>
> Suspense—is his maturer Sister—
> Whether Adult Delight is Pain
> Or of itself a new misgiving—
> This is the Gnat that mangles men—

In this wonder there is a tone of the purest anonymity, as
if the poet, speaking out of her "beautiful but bleak condition," were speaking of our condition as well. Dickinson's
idiom has the startling ring of contemporaneity, like much
of Shakespeare's; she speaks from the interior of a life as we
might imagine ourselves speaking, gifted with genius's au-
dacity and shorn of the merely local and time-bound. If
anonymity is the soul's essential voice—its seductive, mes-
merizing, fatal voice—then Emily Dickinson is our poet of
the soul: our most endlessly fascinating American poet. As
Whitman so powerfully addresses the exterior of American
life, so Dickinson addresses—or has she helped create?—its
unknowable interior.

No one who has read even a few of Dickinson's extraordinary poems can fail to sense the heroic nature of this poet's
quest. It is riddlesome, obsessive, haunting, very often frustrating (to the poet no less than to the reader), but above all
heroic; a romance of epic proportions. For the "poetic enter-
prise" is nothing less than the attempt to realize the soul.
And the attempt to realize the soul (in its muteness, its perfection) is nothing less than the attempt to create a poetry of
transcendence—the kind that outlives its human habitation
and its name.

Dare you see a Soul *at the White Heat?*

Then crouch within the door—
Red—is the Fire's common tint—
But when the vivid Ore
Has vanquished Flame's conditions,
It quivers from the Forge
Without a color, but the light
Of unanointed Blaze.
Least Village has its Blacksmith
Whose Anvil's even ring
Stands symbol for the finger Forge
That soundless tugs—within—
Refining these impatient Ores
With Hammer, and with Blaze
Until the Designated Light
Repudiate the Forge—

Only the soul "at the white heat" achieves the light of "unanointed Blaze"—colorless, soundless, transcendent. This is the triumph of art as well as the triumph of personality, but it is not readily achieved.

Two Selves in Conflict

Very often the "self" is set in opposition to the soul. The personality is mysteriously split, warring: "Of Consciousness, her awful Mate / The Soul cannot be rid—" And: "Me from Myself—to banish— / Had I Art—" A successful work of art is a consequence of the integration of conscious and unconscious elements; a balance of what is known and not quite known held in an exquisite tension. Art *is* tension, and poetry of the kind Emily Dickinson wrote is an art of strain, of nerves strung brilliantly tight. It is compact, dense, coiled in upon itself very nearly to the point of pain: like one of those stellar bodies whose gravity is so condensed it is on the point of disappearing altogether. How tight, how violent, this syntax!—making the reader's heart beat quickly, at times, in sympathy with the poet's heart. By way of Dickinson's radically experimental verse—and, not least, her employment of dashes as punctuation—the drama of the split self is made palpable. One is not merely told of it, one is made to experience it.

Anything less demanding would not be poetry, but prose—the kind of prose written by other people. Though Dickinson was an assured writer of prose herself, "prose" for her assumes a pejorative tone: see the famously rebellious poem in which the predicament of the female (artist? or simply "female"?) is dramatized—

They shut me up in Prose—
As when a little Girl
They put me in the Closet—
Because they liked me "still"—

Still! Could themself have peeped—
And seen my Brain—go round—
They might as wise have lodged a Bird
For Treason—in the Pound—

Himself has but to will
And easy as a Star
Abolish his Captivity—
And laugh—No more have I—

Prose—it might be speculated—is discourse; poetry ellipsis. Prose is spoken aloud; poetry overheard. The one is presumably articulate and social, a shared language, the voice of "communication"; the other is private, allusive, teasing, sly, idiosyncratic as the spider's delicate web, a kind of witchcraft unfathomable to ordinary minds. Poetry, paraphrased, is something other than poetry, while prose *is* paraphrase. Consequently the difficulty of much of Dickinson's poetry, its necessary strategies, for the act of writing is invariably an act of rebellion, a way of (secretly, subversively) "abolishing" captivity:

Tell all the Truth but tell it slant—
Success in Circuit lies
Too bright for our infirm Delight
The Truth's superb surprise
As Lightning to the Children eased
With explanation kind
The Truth must dazzle gradually
Or every man be blind—

Surely there is a witty irony behind the notion that lightning can be domesticated by way of "kind explanations" told to children; that the dazzle of Truth might be gradual and not blinding. The "superb surprise" of which the poet speaks is too much for mankind to bear head-on—like the Medusa it can be glimpsed only indirectly, through the subtly distorting mirror of art.

Elsewhere, in a later poem, the poet suggests a radical distinction between two species of consciousness. Two species of human being?—

Best Witchcraft is Geometry
To the magician's mind—
His ordinary acts are feats
To thinking of mankind.

The "witchcraft" of art is (mere) geometry to the practitioner: by which is meant that it is orderly, natural, obedient to its own rules of logic; an ordinary event. What constitutes the "feat" is the relative ignorance of others—nonmagicians. It is a measure of the poet's modesty that, in this poem and in others, she excludes herself from the practice of witchcraft, even as she brilliantly practices it. Dickinson is most herself when she stands, like us, in awe of her remarkable powers as if sensing how little she controls them; how little, finally, the mute and unknowable Soul has to do with the restless, ever-improvising voice. "Silence," says the poet, "is all we dread. / There's Ransom in a Voice—/ But Silence is Infinity. / Himself have not a face."

A Distinctive Voice

If one were obliged to say what Emily Dickinson's poems as a whole are about, the answer must be ambiguous. The poems are in one sense about the creation of the self capable of creating in turn this very body of poetry. For poetry does not "write itself"—the mind may feed on the heart, but the heart is mute, and requires not only being fed upon but being scrupulously tamed. Like virtually all poets of genius, Emily Dickinson worked hard at her craft. Passion comes unbidden—poetry's flashes of great good luck come unbidden—but the structures into which such flashes are put must be intellectually interesting. For the wisdom of the heart is after all ahistorical—it is always the same wisdom, one might say, across centuries. But human beings live in time, not simply in Time. The historical evolution of one's craft cannot be ignored: in creating art one is always, in a sense, vying for space with preexisting art. Emily Dickinson is perhaps our greatest American poet not because she felt more deeply and more profoundly than other people, or even that she "distilled amazing sense from ordinary Meanings," but that she wrote so well.

Dickinson discovered, early on, her distinctive voice—it is evident in letters written when she was a girl—and worked all her life to make it ever more distinctive. She was the spider, sometimes working at night in the secrecy of her room, unwinding a "Yarn of Pearl" unperceived by others and plying "from Nought to Nought / In unsubstantial Trade—" but she was far more than merely the spider: she is the presence, never directly cited, or even hinted at, who intends to dazzle

the world with her genius. Literary fame is not precisely a
goal, but it *is* a subject to which the poet has given some
thought: "Some—Work for Immortality— / the Chiefer part,
for Time— / "He—Compensates—immediately— / The former—Checks—on Fame—" And, more eloquently in these
late, undated poems that might have been written by an elder
poet who had in fact enjoyed public acclaim:

> Fame is a bee.
>> It has a song—
> It has a sting—
>> Ah, too, it has a
> wing.

And:

> Fame is a fickle food
> Upon a shifting plate
> Whose table once a
> Guest but not
> The second time is set.
>
> Whose crumbs the crows inspect
> And with ironic caw
> Flap past it to the
> Farmer's Corn—
> Men eat of it and die.

Dickinson's specific practice as a writer might strike most
people as haphazard, if not wasteful, but clearly it was the
practice most suited to her temperament and her domestic
situation. During the day, while working at household tasks,
she jotted down sentences or fragments of sentences as they
occurred to her, scribbling on any handy scrap of paper
(which suggests the improvised, unplanned nature of the
process). Later, in her room, she added these scraps to her
scrapbasket collection of phrases, to be "used" when she
wrote poetry or letters. Both Dickinson's poetry and prose,
reading as if they were quickly—breathlessly—imagined,
are the consequence of any number of drafts and revisions.
As biographers have noted, a word or a phrase or a striking
image might be worked into a poem or a letter years after it
was first written down: the motive even in the private correspondence is to create a persona, not to speak spontaneously. And surely, after a point, it was not possible for
Dickinson to speak except by way of a persona.

A Difficult Poet to Know

Helen McNeil

When confronted by a truly unusual poet such as Dickinson, critics must often reexamine their ideas of what makes a poem great or even good. With no standard by which to make comparisons, Dickinson's work was often misinterpreted and misunderstood by early readers who simply were not sophisticated enough to transcend the conventions of the day. In the following article, Helen McNeil attempts to define Dickinson on her own terms.

McNeil, who received her Ph.D. from Yale, wrote her study *Emily Dickinson* while lecturer at the University of East Anglia, not far from her subject's birthplace. It was written in the centenary year of Emily Dickinson's death.

Emily Dickinson (1830–86) was one of the indispensable poets in English; one of the very greatest English poets. Her accomplishment is so radically original that the entire model of what poetry can know (and write) changes when her work is taken into account. And when our sense of writing changes, our entire model of knowledge shifts. Emily Dickinson was a woman; she wrote consciously and with profound insight about her womanly life. If we who read her are women, her accomplishment enlarges our recognition of ourselves.

The poetry of Emily Dickinson was virtually unknown during her lifetime, although she wrote almost 1,800 poems and fragments. Since then, Dickinson has gradually gained acceptance as an important lyric poet, though her range has often been considered limited. Some of her more cheerful lyrics have been standard anthology poems in the United States for many years, thus inadvertently disguising her clarity and fierceness. A collected *Poems* finally appeared in 1955, and her rich and demanding letters were published in

From Helen McNeil, *Emily Dickinson* (London: Virago Press, 1986). Copyright ©1986 by Helen McNeil. Reprinted by permission of the publisher.

1958. Dickinson's poetry is now readily available in paperback, and specialist studies have begun to flood from the presses. One recent study begins by describing Dickinson as the finest American woman poet.

Emily Dickinson was indeed American, and proudly so; she was a middle-class New England woman, well educated in terms of the prevailing cultural norms. In 'The Robin's my Criterion for Tune—' she wrote that 'Because I see—New Englandly', even a queen in one of her poems 'discerns like me—/Provincially—'. There is some irony in the way Dickinson is using 'provincial' in that last line. Dickinson did not consider American literature to be provincial. Also, anyone who writes accurately must write from experience, from their own province. Dickinson's poetry is set in that immediate moment of existence, with little nostalgia for a more overtly poetic medieval past.

Dickinson's kind of excellence, her kind of womanliness and the kind of poet she was are all, however, much less self-evident. One function of Dickinson's accomplishment is to force us to reconsider what we understand by greatness, gender and poetic knowledge. By coming to know her, we come to know them in a different way. . . .

CHANGES ASSUMPTIONS OF GREATNESS

It is, in fact, easy not to know Emily Dickinson. Because she is such an original writer, she has tended to be described according to what she is not: not a man, not like Walt Whitman, not 'professional', not normal, and not married. A writer who is described as different from what we know is bound to seem difficult. A writer who is said to come from a group whose limitations we think we know—an old maid American Victorian recluse poet, for example—is going to look limited.

It is easy not to know Dickinson because the type she manifests—the great woman poet—is still in the root sense not known by our culture. And whenever there is ignorance, there are reasons why ignorance has settled in that particular spot. I also do not know Dickinson fully. Whenever I open her *Complete Poems* I find her describing some new state or arguing some new premise or pioneering some new use of language. I have also had to find my way out of assuming that because I am a woman I would know automatically what Dickinson would think, and accept instead the surprise of what she truly thinks. Emily Dickinson has a lot to teach us, not least when she offers her awesomely accurate inside pictures of taboo subjects such as fear, hopeless longing, dread, death and loss.

FROM A LETTER TO T.W. HIGGINSON

Published after Dickinson's death in Letters of Emily Dickinson, *this letter to T.W. Higginson responds to the editor's criticism of her work. Though she acknowledges Higginson's opinion of her unconventional style, Dickinson is clearly aware of her own potential for greatness.*

If fame belonged to me, I could not escape her; if she did not, the longest day would pass me on the chase, and the approbation of my dog would forsake me then. My barefoot rank is better.

You think my gait "spasmodic." I am in danger, sir. You think me "uncontrolled." I have no tribunal.

Would you have time to be the "friend" you should think I need? I have a little shape: it would not crowd your desk, nor make much racket as the mouse that dents your galleries.

For the non-academic reader, the many points where Dickinson diverges from literary tradition have little importance. Dickinson is a very direct writer, and the emotional tenor and major themes of her poems reveal themselves easily. Typically, she begins a poem with a powerful recognition:

It was not Death, for I stood up,
And all the Dead, lie down—
It was not Night, for all the Bells
Put out their Tongues, for Noon.

This imagery is complex and quick-changing, with a surreal image of church bells sticking out their tongues coming hard upon the eerie picture of the speaker as perhaps a vertical corpse. Yet the tone is unmistakeable—a nightmarish, fixed terror mixed with a curiously calm investigatory interest.

Even though her works have only gradually filtered through to a large public, there is a genuinely popular element to Dickinson. It is those trained in critical theory who find Dickinson 'different', because she doesn't fit a received model for literary greatness. I believe Dickinson's poetry changes literary theory. To think about how Dickinson wrote is to experience gaps and silences in the existing models. Reading her fully means redefining those models. It is an exhilarating sensation.

Dickinson's Need for Seclusion

Adrienne Rich

Critic, essayist, and feminist, Adrienne Rich is best
known as a poet. In 1974 Rich shared the National
Book Award with poet Allen Ginsberg. Her poems
"Aunt Jennifer's Tigers" and "Diving into the Wreck"
are among the most widely anthologized poems of
our time. This excerpt from her essay "Vesuvius at
Home: The Power of Emily Dickinson" is a medita-
tion on the life and work of a poet Rich calls a
genius. It begins in the first person with the author
making a drive to Dickinson's old homestead.

I am travelling at the speed of time, along the Massachusetts
Turnpike. For months, for years, for most of my life, I have
been hovering like an insect against the screens of an existence which inhabited Amherst, Massachusetts, between
1831 and 1884. The methods, the exclusions, of Emily Dickinson's existence could not have been my own; yet more and
more, as a woman poet finding my own methods, I have
come to understand her necessities, could have been witness in her defense.

"Home is not where the heart is," she wrote in a letter,
"but the house and the adjacent buildings." A statement of
New England realism, a directive to be followed. Probably
no poet ever lived so much and so purposefully in one
house; even, in one room. Her niece Martha told of visiting
her in her corner bedroom on the second floor at 280 Main
Street, Amherst, and of how Emily Dickinson made as if to
lock the door with an imaginary key, turned and said:
"Matty: here's freedom."

I am travelling at the speed of time, in the direction of the
house and buildings.

Western Massachusetts: the Connecticut Valley: a coun-

Excerpted from "Vesuvius at Home: The Power of Emily Dickinson," in *On Lies,
Secrets, and Silence: Selected Prose, 1966–1978* by Adrienne Rich. Copyright ©1979 by
W.W. Norton & Company, Inc. Reprinted by permission of the author and W.W. Norton
& Company, Inc.

tryside still full of reverberations: scene of Indian uprisings, religious revivals, spiritual confrontations, the blazing-up of the lunatic fringe of the Puritan coal. How peaceful and how threatened it looks from Route 91, hills gently curled above the plain, the tobacco-barns standing in fields sheltered with white gauze from the sun, and the sudden urban sprawl: ARCO, McDonald's, shopping plazas. The country that broke the heart of Jonathan Edwards, that enclosed the genius of Emily Dickinson. It lies calmly in the light of May, cloudy skies breaking into warm sunshine, light-green spring softening the hills, dogwood and wild fruit-trees blossoming in the hollows.

From Northhampton bypass there's a 4-mile stretch of road to Amherst—Route 9—between fruit farms, steakhouses, supermarkets. The new University of Massachusetts rears its skyscrapers up from the plain against the Pelham Hills. There is new money here, real estate, motels. Amherst succeeds on Hadley almost without notice. Amherst is green, rich-looking, secure; we're suddenly in the center of town, the crossroads of the campus, old New England college buildings spread around two village greens, a scene I remember as almost exactly the same in the dim past of my undergraduate years when I used to come there for college weekends.

Left on Seelye Street, right on Main; driveway at the end of a yellow picket fence. I recognize the high hedge of cedars screening the house, because twenty-five years ago I walked there, even then drawn toward the spot, trying to peer over. I pull into the driveway behind a generous 19th-century brick mansion with wings and porches, old trees and green lawns. I ring at the back door—the door through which Dickinson's coffin was carried to the cemetery a block away.

A JUSTIFICATION FOR SECLUSION

For years I have been not so much envisioning Emily Dickinson as trying to visit, to enter her mind, through her poems and letters, and through my own intimations of what it could have meant to be one of the two mid–19th-century American geniuses, and a woman, living in Amherst, Massachusetts. Of the other genius, Walt Whitman, Dickinson wrote that she had heard his poems were "disgraceful." She knew her own were unacceptable by her world's standards of poetic convention, and of what was appropriate, in partic-

"E."

*Though Dickinson was seen by some, including her editor
T.W. Higginson, as slightly crazy, poet Adrienne Rich views
Dickinson's life choices as not only deliberate but necessary to
the creation of her work. In this poem, found in Albert Gelpi's*
Emily Dickinson: The Mind of a Poet, *Rich portrays Dickinson's solitary life as its own response to Higginson and others
who were unable to appreciate Dickinson on her own terms.*

'Halfcracked' to Higginson, living,
afterward famous in garbled versions–
your hoard of dazzling scraps a battlefield–
now your old snood

mothballed at Harvard
and you in your variorum monument
equivocal to the end–
who are you?

Gardening the day-lily,
wiping the wine-glass stems,
your thought pulsed on behind
a forehead battered paper-thin,

you, woman, masculine
in singlemindedness,
for whom the word was more
than a symptom–

a condition of being.
Till the air buzzing with spoiled language
sang in your ears
of Perjury

and in your halfcracked way you chose
silence for entertainment,
chose to have it out at last
on your own premises.

ular, for a woman poet. Seven were published in her lifetime,
all edited by other hands; more than a thousand were laid
away in her bedroom chest, to be discovered after her death.
When her sister discovered them, there were decades of
struggle over the manuscripts, the manner of their presentation to the world, their suitability for publication, the poet's
own final intentions. Narrowed-down by her early editors
and anthologists, reduced to quaintness or spinsterish odd-

ity by many of her commentators, sentimentalized, fallen-in-love with like some gnomic Garbo, still unread in the breadth and depth of her full range of work, she was, and is, a wonder to me when I try to imagine myself into that mind.

I have a notion that genius knows itself; that Dickinson chose her seclusion, knowing she was exceptional and knowing what she needed. It was, moreover, no hermetic retreat, but a seclusion which included a wide range of people, of reading and correspondence. Her sister Vinnie said, "Emily is always looking for the rewarding person." And she found, at various periods, both women and men: her sister-in-law Susan Gilbert, Amherst visitors and family friends such as Benjamin Newton, Charles Wadsworth, Samuel Bowles, editor of the Springfield *Republican* and his wife; her friends Kate Anthon and Helen Hunt Jackson, the distant but significant figures of Elizabeth Barrett, the Brontës, George Eliot. But she carefully selected her society and controlled the disposal of her time. Not only the "gentlewoman in plush" of Amherst were excluded; Emerson visited next door but she did not go to meet him; she did not travel or receive routine visits; she avoided strangers. Given her vocation, she was neither eccentric nor quaint; she was determined to survive, to use her powers, to practice necessary economies. . . .

Upstairs at last: I stand in the room which for Emily Dickinson was "freedom." The best bedroom in the house, a corner room, sunny, overlooking the main street of Amherst in front, the way to her brother Austin's house on the side. Here, at a small table with one drawer, she wrote most of her poems. Here she read Elizabeth Barrett's "Aurora Leigh," a woman poet's narrative poem of a woman poet's life; also George Eliot; Emerson; Carlyle; Shakespeare; Charlotte and Emily Brontë. Here I become, again, an insect, vibrating at the frames of windows, clinging to panes of glass, trying to connect. The scent here is very powerful. Here in this white-curtained, high-ceilinged room, a redhaired woman with hazel eyes and a contralto voice wrote poems about volcanoes, deserts, eternity, suicide, physical passion, wild beasts, rape, power, madness, separation, the daemon, the grave. Here, with a darning-needle, she bound these poems—heavily emended and often in variant versions—into booklets, secured with darning-thread, to be found and read after her death. Here she knew "freedom," listening from above-stairs to a visitor's piano-playing, escaping from the pantry where she was mistress of the household bread and puddings, watching, you feel, watching ceaselessly, the life of sober Main Street below. From this room she glided downstairs, her hand on the polished bannister, to meet the complacent magazine editor, Thomas Higginson, unnerve him while claiming she herself was unnerved. "Your scholar," she signed herself in letters to him. But she was an independent scholar, used his criticism selectively, saw him rarely and always on *her* premises. It was a life deliberately organized on her terms. The terms she had been handed by society— Calvinist Protestantism, Romanticism, the 19th-century corseting of women's bodies, choices, and sexuality—could spell insanity to a woman genius. What this one had to do was retranslate into a dialect called metaphor: her native language. "Tell all the Truth—but tell it Slant—." It is always what is under pressure in us, especially under pressure of concealment—that explodes in poetry.

Dickinson Was Misunderstood by Those Closest to Her

Amy Lowell

Amy Lowell was an American poet, critic, and biographer who became a leader of the Imagist movement of the early 1900s. The Imagists sought to break poetry out of the restrictive meter and stiff diction pioneered by English writers such as William Wordsworth. The poetry of the Imagists tended to be short, written in free verse, and constructed around a single, spectacular metaphor. Their influence is still apparent in contemporary poetry.

Lowell, who was known as much for her cigar smoking and outspoken nature as for her writing, lived a very different life than her subject. In this excerpt she laments Dickinson's isolation and obscurity as much as she praises the highly original vision of her predecessor.

I wonder what made Emily Dickinson as she was. She cannot be accounted for by any trick of ancestry or early influence. She was the daughter of a long line of worthy people; her father, who was the leading lawyer of Amherst, Massachusetts, and the treasurer of Amherst College, is typical of the aims and accomplishments of the race. Into this well-ordered, high-minded, average, and rather sombre milieu, swept Emily Dickinson like a beautiful, stray butterfly, 'beating in the void her luminous wings in vain.' She knew no different life; and yet she certainly did not belong to the one in which she found herself. She may have felt this in some obscure fashion; for, little by little, she withdrew from the world about her, and shut herself up in a cocoon of her own spinning. She had no heart to fight; she never knew that a battle was on and that she had been selected for a place in the vanguard; all she could do was to retire, to hide her wounds, to carry out her little skirmishings and advances in byways and side-tracks, slowly winning a territory which the enemy took no trouble to dispute. What she did seemed insignificant and individual, but thirty years after her death the flag under which she fought had become a great banner, the symbol of a militant revolt. It is an odd story, this history of Imagism, and perhaps the oddest and saddest moment in it is comprised in the struggle of this one brave, fearful, and unflinching woman.

There is very little to tell about Emily Dickinson's life. In a sense, she had no life except that of the imagination. Born in Amherst in December, 1830, she died there in May, 1886. Her travels consisted of occasional trips to Boston, and one short sojourn in Washington during her father's term in Congress. As the years went on, she could scarcely be induced to leave her own threshold; what she saw from her window, what she read in her books, were her only external *stimuli.* Those few people whom she admitted to her friendship were loved with the terrible and morbid exaggeration of the profoundly lonely. In this isolation, all resilience to the blows of illness and death was atrophied. She could not take up her life again because there was no life to take. Her thoughts came to be more and more preoccupied with the grave. Her letters were painful reading indeed to the normal-minded. Here was a woman with a nice wit, a sparkling sense of humour, sinking under the weight of an introverted imagination to a state bordering upon neurasthenia; for her horror of publicity would not certainly be classed as a 'phobia.' The ignorance and unwisdom of her friends confused illness with genius, and, reversing the usual experience in such cases, they saw in the morbidness of hysteria, the sensitiveness of a peculiarly artistic nature. In the introduction to the collection of her letters, the editor, Mrs. Mabel Loomis Todd, says, 'In her later years, Emily Dickinson rarely addressed the envelopes; it seemed as if her sensitive nature shrank from the publicity which even her handwriting would undergo, in the observation of indifferent eyes. Various expedients were resorted to—obliging friends frequently performed this office for her; sometimes a printed newspaper label was pasted upon the envelope; but the actual strokes of her own pencil were, so far as possible, reserved exclusively for friendly eyes.'

That is no matter for laughter, but for weeping. What loneliness, disappointment, misunderstanding must have preceded it! What unwise protection against the clear, buffeting winds of life must have been exerted to shut the poor

"THE SISTERS"

Originally published in 1925, Amy Lowell's poem "The Sisters" asks why Lowell and women like her write poetry. In this excerpt, which appears in The Complete Poetical Works of Amy Lowell, *Lowell praises Dickinson over such famous poets as Sappho and Elizabeth Barrett Browning.*

. . . I go dreaming on,
In love with these my spiritual relations.
I rather think I see myself walk up
A flight of wooden steps and ring a bell
And send a card in to Miss Dickinson.
Yet that's a very silly way to do.
I should have taken the dream twist-ends about
And climbed over the fence and found her deep
Engrossed in the doing of a hummingbird
Among nasturtiums. Not having expected strangers,
She might forget to think me one, and holding up
A finger say quite casually: "Take care.
Don't frighten him, he's only just begun."
"Now this," I well believe I should have thought,
"Is even better than Sappho. With Emily
You're really here, or never anywhere at all
In range of mind." Wherefore, having begun
In the strict centre, we could slowly progress
To various circumferences, as we pleased.
We could, but should we? That would quite depend
On Emily. I think she'd be exacting,
Without intention possibly, and ask
A thousand tight-rope tricks of understanding.
But, bless you, I would somersault all day
If by so doing I might stay with her.
I hardly think that we should mention souls
Although they might just round the corner from us
In some half-quizzical, half-wistful metaphor.
I'm very sure that I should never seek
To turn her parables to stated fact.
Sappho would speak, I think, quite openly,
And Mrs. Browning guard a careful silence,
But Emily would set doors ajar and slam them
And love you for your speed of observation.

soul into her stifling hot-house! The times were out of joint
for Emily Dickinson. Her circle loved her, but utterly failed
to comprehend. Her daring utterances shocked; her whim-
sicality dazed. The account of this narrow life is heart-
rending. Think of Charles Lamb joking a New England dea-
con; imagine Keats's letters read aloud to a Dorcas Society;
conceive of William Blake sending the 'Songs of Experience'
to the 'Springfield Republican'! Emily Dickinson lived in an
atmosphere of sermons, church sociables, and county newspapers. It is ghastly, the terrible, inexorable waste of Nature,
but it is a fact. The direct descendant of Blake (although she
probably never heard of him) lived in this surrounding. The
marvel is that her mind did not give way. It did not; except
in so far as her increasing shrinking from society and her
preoccupation with death may be considered giving way.
She lived on; she never ceased to write; and the torture
which she suffered must have been exquisite indeed.

SMALL ATTEMPTS AT RECOGNITION THWARTED

Whenever a little door opened, some kind friend immediately slammed it to. Her old school companion Mrs. Jackson,
better known as H.H., the author of 'Ramona,' repeatedly
begged her to write for the 'No Name Series,' then just starting. And the poet whom everybody deemed so retiring was
half inclined to accept. She needed to be pushed into the
healthy arena of publicity, a little assistance over the bump
of her own shyness and a new, bright, and vigorous life
would have lain before her. In an evil moment she asked the
advice of Mr. Thomas Wentworth Higginson. The very words
of her letter show her half pleading to be urged on:

> Dear Friend:
>   Are you willing to tell me what is right? Mrs. Jackson, of
> Colorado, was with me a few moments this week, and wished
> me to write for this. I told her I was unwilling, and she asked
> me why? I said I was incapable, and she seemed not to be-
> lieve me and asked me not to decide for a few days. Meantime
> she would write to me. . . . I would regret to estrange her, and
> if you would be willing to give me a note saying you disap-
> proved it and thought me unfit, she would believe you.

The disapproval was cordially given; the door shut again
upon the prisoner, who thanks her jailor with the least hint
of regret between the lines:

> Dear Friend:
>   . . . I am glad I did as you would like. The degradation to

displease you, I hope I may never incur.

Mild, sweet-tempered, sympathetic, and stupid Mr. Higginson! It was an evil moment when Emily chose him for the arbiter of her fate. And yet who, at the time, would have done better? Certainly not Longfellow, nor Lowell, nor Emerson. Poe? But Emily could not write to a man like Poe. Whitman? She herself says in another letter to her mentor, 'You speak of Mr. Whitman. I never read his book, but was told that it was disgraceful.'

No, there was no hope. All her friends were in the conspiracy of silence. They could not believe that the public was made up of many people as sensitive as themselves. Mrs. Gordon L. Ford has related an interesting anecdote illustrative of this point of view. I will give it in her own words:

> Dr. Holland once said to me, 'Her poems are too ethereal for publication.' I replied. 'They are beautiful—so concentrated——but they remind me of air-plants that have no roots in earth.' 'That is true,' he said, 'a perfect description;' and I think these lyrical ejaculations, these breathed-out projectiles, sharp as lances, would at that time have fallen into idle ears.

And yet when her first volume was published posthumously, it went through six editions in as many months.

The truth is that, as someone once said to me, the average man is a good deal above the average. A fact which the newly awakened interest in poetry is proving every day. This same first edition was published in 1890, more than twenty years before Imagism as a distinct school was heard of, but its reception shows that the soil was already ripe for sowing.

Why Emily Dickinson Wore White

Kathryn Whitford

The responsibility of housework in the nineteenth century was a tremendous burden to Emily Dickinson, who wrote about her chores in letters to friends and family. Clothing of various colors and patterns was difficult to clean and sew and took a certain amount of mental energy to coordinate, update, and keep seasonal. Dickinson scholar Kathryn Whitford believes that to Emily Dickinson, who had little use for fashion, these chores were distractions from her writing. Whitford speculates that Dickinson's mysterious white dresses were nothing more than a practical convenience.

In classrooms and in discussion with readers of Emily Dickinson's poetry, one hears not only that she withdrew from the world, but that in response to an unrequited love she wore only "bridal white" during the last decades of her life. Her choice of white has served as the capstone to arguments setting forth her mental or emotional frailties. The time has come to recognize that although she chose to wear white she almost certainly did not think of it as "bridal."

Millicent Todd Bingham prefaced her book *Emily Dickinson's Home* with the hope that the work would "replace queerness with reasonableness as an explanation of Emily Dickinson's conduct." Her argument that keeping a large house without central heating, without gas or electricity and without running water, so occupied Emily's time that she was forced to retire from the social life of the community in order to find time for her poetry has gradually been accepted by the academic community; but the myth of "bridal white" persists. In the hope of once again replacing "queerness with reasonableness" this paper will place Emily's

Kathryn Whitford, "Why Emily Dickinson Wore White," *Dickinson Studies*, no. 55, 1985. Reprinted by permission of the author.

white dresses in their proper nineteenth-century context.

Emily Dickinson and her friends would not have associated white exclusively with "bridal" because congregational weddings of her day were usually simpler affairs than they have since become. A wedding gown was not then a costume for a single day, but a dress that could be worn for other events. It might be white, but it might also be gray or mauve, or, for a winter wedding, even brown or navy. Moreover, white was a common color for summer dresses for girls and young women. The chief argument against Emily's "bridal white," however, lies not in the marriage customs of the day but in the rigors of nineteenth-century housekeeping and laundry.

THE EXPECTATION OF LABOR

About January of 1856, after the family had moved into the Dickinson homestead, Mrs. Dickinson was in ill health and as Emily wrote to Mrs. J.G. Holland, "Vinnie and I 'regulated' and Vinnie and I 'got settled' and still we keep our father's house and mother lies upon the lounge." Mrs. Dickinson's invalidism continued for several years, throwing the burden of housekeeping upon her daughters. The house was large and the family, although they employed an ironing woman and a washerwoman by the day, did not keep live-in household help until the early sixties when the Irish housegirl named Margaret O'Brien was hired. Even with the addition of a maid-of-all-work, household tasks probably consumed more of Dickinson's time than has been recognized by anyone except Mrs. Bingham. Thomas Johnson wrote that "like her mother and unlike her sister, Lavinia was willing to undertake responsibility for routine domestic affairs." Careful reading of Emily's letters supports Mrs. Bingham's argument that Emily was actively involved in the domestic duties of the household.

Three times in the 1850s Dickinson wrote that she had made up the fires and prepared breakfast and then, because the rest of the family was not yet awake, she was seizing the brief quiet time to write her letter. In 1864, when Margaret O'Brien left the household and Margaret Maher had not yet been hired, Dickinson wrote Mrs. Holland that "Besides wiping the dishes for Margaret, I wash them now, while she becomes Mrs. Lawler." Other references to dishes suggest that wiping dishes was one of Dickinson's tasks even when domestic help was present. No housemaid remained long in the Dickinson service during the four years after Margaret O'Brien's marriage, so it seems probable that Emily washed and wiped the dishes from many meals. The Dickinson women had their dresses cut and sometimes made by professional sewingwomen of the town, but they were clearly responsible for making their own intimate garments such as petticoats, nightgowns, robes, etc. In 1859 Emily wrote, "I am sewing for Vinnie." In December, 1861, a letter notes, "Took up my work hemming strings for mother's gown." In 1863, "I finished mama's saque, all but the overcasting." Thomas Wentworth Higginson's letter to his wife (Aug. 16, 1870) states that Emily "makes all the bread for her father likes only hers," a statement confirmed by Ellen E. Dickinson, the wife of Emily's cousin Willie, who wrote in 1890 that Emily "was a past mistress of cookery and housekeeping. She made desserts for the household dinners; delicious confections and bread." One begins to wonder how she had time to be a poet.

It is against this background that one must see not only her withdrawal from society but her adoption of white dresses. Millicent Todd Bingham says that Dickinson's retirement came not because she shunned people but because "she wanted time" and that she made no decision to withdraw but was "drawn into an inch-by-inch retirement quite apart from any hypothetical heartbreak." Thomas Johnson characterizes Dickinson's rejection of society as "her kind of economy, a frugality she sought in order to make the most of her world."

The white dresses were probably also an "inch-by-inch" approach to her frugality with time. It is unlikely that a serviceable dress was discarded in such a household. But at some point Dickinson must have made a deliberate decision to replace her dresses only with white ones. In a letter of about 1860 she wrote Lavinia Norcross, "My sphere is doubtless calicoes, nevertheless I thought it meet to sport a little wool. The mirth it has occasioned will deter me from further exhibitions." The letter suggests that Dickinson is already wearing chiefly cotton dresses appropriate for housework and baking. She would need her plain brown wool less and less as she ceased to leave the house and grounds. It was the calicoes and ginghams that gave place to white dresses.

There is no hint of a washerwoman after the advent of the first of the housegirls to the Dickinson household; on the other hand there are indications that the washing and iron-ing were now household functions. Although the heavy wash, household linens, etc., was undoubtedly performed by the domestic, the care of their own dresses would ordinarily have been the responsibility of the women of the household, if only because the caution required in washing colored fab-rics and calicoes could not be entrusted safely to a maid-of-all-work. Dickinson's letter to Louise and Fanny Norcross suggests, however, that she as well as Maggie was busy on washday. The family was expecting a visit from Edward Dickinson's formidable sister Elizabeth, and Emily wrote, "I hoped she'd come while you were here to help me with the starch," apparently for the pillowcases.

A PRACTICAL DECISION

The problems and extra work connected with washing col-ored cottons, and particularly calicoes, stemmed from the fact that few nineteenth-century dyes were stable. Old veg-etable dyes had given a genuinely fast turkey red and log-wood black, but neither color was suitable for the Dickinson women. Other dyes were sunfast but not waterfast, or the other way around. The tan, brown and olive colors in gen-eral use were so fugitive that Catherine Beecher in her *Trea-tise on Domestic Economy* recommended washing dresses of those colors in a hay infusion to preserve the colors, or, in truth, to restore the color lost in washing. It was not until the introduction of modern vat colors, after 1914, that commer-cially dyed fabrics could be expected to hold their colors. Even then, as Charles E. Pellew comments in his volume *Dyes and Dyeing,*

> The extra cost of the dyestuffs and the difficulty of dyeing to shade, furnish an excuse for increasing the price of the goods. And the perhaps not unnatural disinclination of shopkeepers to push the sale of materials which, in their opinion, are quite unnecessarily fast, has combined to delay the general adop-tion of these remarkably valuable coloring agents.

Earlier he had fulminated that "a calico dress which keeps its color so that it can be worn for a second summer, is an abomination not to be endured" by greedy merchants. Pellew's comment goes far toward explaining the succession of poor heroines in "faded calico" marching across the pages of nineteenth-century fiction. It also explains Catherine Beecher's elaborate instructions for washing calico or other colored cottons.

Such fabrics were never to be boiled or washed in very warm water. They were never to be "left long in the water" or permitted to remain crumpled or folded while wet as it "injures the colors." Translated that means that the dyes would run. For the same reason the water in which they were washed was to be changed "whenever it appears dingy, or the light parts will look dirty." They must not be rubbed with soap, but grease should be removed with "French chalk, starch, magnesia or Wilmington clay." Colored dresses were to be dried, inside out, in the shade and never allowed to freeze. Catherine Beecher further suggested that the starch for calicoes be made with coffee water because ordinary white starch would leave a faint bloom on the dark colors. The alternative was to starch calicoes with glue dissolved in an appropriate quantity of water.

Miss Beecher comments that some people washed calicoes without soap, in bran water, "four quarts of wheat-bran to two pails of water," and followed by rinsing in bran water. How they then got the bran out of the clothes she doesn't say, but a more extended rule for the same method was still being printed in 1903. As an afterthought Miss Beecher adds that potato water is equally good, "take eight peeled and grated potatoes to one gallon of water."

By comparison, washing white items was easy. The wash was sorted into coarse whites and fine whites, or one assumes, the equivalent of household linens and family undergarments. Both classes were soaked overnight and then boiled (two hours for coarse whites, half an hour for fine whites), washed with potash soap, rinsed, starched and hung out to dry in the sun. Potash soap was a mild bleaching agent, the forerunner of the washing soda still on the market. Chlorine bleaching powder had been invented before 1800 and was available by the middle of the nineteenth century, but Miss Beecher does not mention it, preferring the potash soap for which she supplies a recipe, adding that since the soap improves with age it would be well to make "two barrels at once." She also recommends mild lye solutions for bleaching natural linen, and salt, lemon juice, and buttermilk for removing stains resistant to boiling.

It is against this background of housekeeping practices that one must examine what is recorded about the poet's dresses after she began staying home. Her dressmaker and her neighbors were unanimous in testifying that Emily wore only white. Yet as late as 1870 white seems to have had no esoteric significance for her. When T.W. Higginson called upon her, she was obviously keyed up and determined to make her best impression. She entered the room in her customary white gown, but with Lavinia's blue net shawl about her shoulders. In other words, she did not categorically wear only white; she wore only white dresses. Higginson described her gown as piqué, immaculately clean. Later Eugene Field, who had been a neighbor of the Dickinsons in his youth, described her white dresses as simple almost to severity.

Looking closely at the scraps of evidence available after nearly one hundred years, it becomes clear that because the withdrawal and the white gowns were both efforts to gain time for herself, Emily's choice of white was clear-headed and practical. Her dresses were the farthest removed from bridal finery. They were in fact, more nearly a uniform. The uniform was white for the same reason that the uniforms of doctors, nurses, cooks and butchers were white, which in turn was the same reason that nineteenth-century sheets and towels, pillowcases and table linen were uncompromisingly white. White linen and cotton were the easiest fabrics to wash. So long as Dickinson wore white dresses she did not have to cope with the special demands of calico or other colored fabrics. Even better, her white dresses, like her petticoats, could be added to the household wash of "fine whites" to be soaked and boiled by the maid-of-all-work and starched in the same tub with petticoats and pillowcases. The simplicity of the dresses insured that there would be small need of fluting irons whether used by herself or Maggie, of whom she wrote in 1870, "Maggie is ironing, and a cotton and linen and ruffle heat make the [girl's] cheeks red."

The authors of *The American Woman's Home* proposed to solve the problems of washing and ironing by the establishment of neighborhood laundries where "one or two women could do in fine style what now is very indifferently done by the disturbance and disarrangement of all other domestic processes in these families. Whoever set neighborhood-laundries on foot will do much to solve the American housekeeper's hardest problem." By wearing white dresses Emily Dickinson solved the problem for herself. She simplified her living and gained time for poetry and her intense inner life.

Dickinson Found Significance in Minor Events

Ella Gilbert Ives

In this excerpt from a 1907 essay first published in the *Boston Transcript*, poet and teacher Ella Gilbert Ives responds to early critics of Dickinson with wit and sensitivity. While she concedes that Dickinson's rhymes are often imperfect, her rhythms jolting, Ives makes the case that Dickinson forged a new style in measuring a voice so unique she compares it to "the first bullet."

In an attempt to appropriately evaluate Dickinson's poetic sensibility, Ives turns to the life of the poet: her family, her surroundings, and her literary influences. She also looks at Dickinson's relationship with Thomas W. Higginson, who coedited Dickinson's *Poems* after her death.

"If fame belonged to me, I could not escape her."

Emily Dickinson long eluded her pursuer; but no sooner had she left her chrysalis than Fame, also a winged elf, flew by her side, became her unescapable companion. In life she was arrogantly shy of a public that now shares her innermost confidence, and touches with rude or hallowed finger the flesh of her sensitive poetry; the soul of it, happily only the sympathetic can reach.

Many obvious, many contradictory things, have been said about this profound thinker and virile writer on a few great themes. Those who cling to the old order and regard perfect form essential to greatness, have had their fling at her eccentricities, her blemishes, her crudities; they place her with the purveyors of raw material to the artistic producers of the race. They deny her rank with the creators of permanent

From Ella Gilbert Ives, "Emily Dickinson: Her Poetry, Prose, and Personality," *Boston Transcript*, October 5, 1907.

beauty and value. Others such as hail a Wagner, a Whitman, or a Turner, as an originator of new types and a contributor of fresh streams of life blood to art or literature, accept Emily Dickinson as another proof of Nature's fecundity, versatility and daring. All acknowledge in her elements of power and originality; but especially a certain probing quality that penetrates and discloses like an X-ray.

By long-accepted standards, doubtless, she does not measure up to greatness. The first bullet was an innovation to one who drew the long bow. He did not know what to make of hot shot without the whiz and the grace of the arrow—least of all when it struck home and shattered his pet notions. Emily Dickinson's power of condensation, the rhythmic hammer of her thoughts, whether in prose or verse, is so phenomenal that it calls for a new system of weights and measures. Perhaps there is nothing essentially new here. Franklin merely identified an acquaintance of Noah's when he flew his kite; Newton, had he talked the apple over with Eve, might have found her intelligent on the fall; but both philosophers drew as near to originality as mortal is ever permitted to draw by the jealous gods. Emily Dickinson, whatever her size, is of nobody's kind but her own. . . .

No art can be adequately understood apart from the artist. Emily Dickinson is the best commentary upon her verse. I have recently visited "the house behind the hedge," where she was born and died. I have stood in the old-fashioned garden where she strolled, and grew intimate with bird and bee, butterfly and flower. I have listened to her bluebird, who

> Shouts for joy to nobody
> But his seraphic self,

and seen her robin brood its young. I have looked across her landscape on a June day at the Pelham range and repeated:

> The skies can't keep their secret,
> They tell it to the hills.

And letting thought and feeling slip in her accustomed grooves, I have ceased to wonder that Emily Dickinson shut herself in behind that austere but tonic hemlock hedge, and made her house a nunnery. I seemed to hear her voice saying:

> The soul selects her own society
> Then shuts the door;
> On her divine majority
> Obtrude no more.

The events of Emily Dickinson's life are singularly few,

but she invests each with significance. Her perception is at times as vivid as if, called to die, she were taking a last look. Deep and powerful are the strokes with which she limns an emotion, as if she were standing at a judgment bar. If the adjective "intense" were not so overworked, I should employ it. Had Emily Dickinson written novels they would have had the Brontëan quality—flame. A friend tells me that during the later years of her life the poet was accustomed to keep a candle burning in her window at night for the belated traveller. It is symbolic of her genius.

It is the brevity and searching quality (in inverse ratio) of Emily Dickinson's poetry that render it unique, and augur permanence, not so much that it lights the pathway, as that it explores the heart and touches the quick of experience. Her verse is never didactic, yet always earnest; too serious for wit, yet having the very kernel of wit—surprise—to an extraordinary degree. This dressing up of the primal emotions in strange, often outlandish garb, or exhibiting them naked yet not ashamed, has a singular effect, and throws the mind back with questioning upon the writer herself, and the influences that made her what she was—the loneliest figure in the world of letters.

They are not far to seek. There was the mother, whom "Noah would have liked," and the father, who stepped "like Cromwell, when he gets the kindlings." She sketches both saliently: "Mother drives with Tim to carry pears to settlers. Sugar pears with hips like hams, and the flesh of bonbons. ... Father is growing better, though physically reluctant.... You know he never played, and the straightest engine has its leaning hour." To [her friend and mentor Colonel Thomas W.] Higginson she wrote: "My mother does not care for thought, and father, too busy with his briefs to notice what we do. He buys me many books, and begs me not to read them, because he fears they joggle the mind." To another friend she wrote: "Mother is very fond of flowers and of recollection, that sweetest flower."

To Colonel Higginson she talked much about her father—a man who "read on Sunday lonely and rigorous books"; and so inspired her with awe that she did not learn to tell time until fifteen years old, because he had tried to explain it to her when a little child, and she was afraid to tell him she did not understand; also afraid to ask anyone else lest he should hear of it. He did not wish his children when young to read anything but the Bible. But at least two books early ran the blockade: *Kavanagh*, brought home by her brother, was hidden under the piano cover; and Lydia Maria Child's *Letters from New York*, sent by a friend, found refuge in a box beside the doorstep. . . .

She had earlier written to Colonel Higginson: "You inquire my books? For poets, I have Keats and Mr. and Mrs. Browning. For prose, Mr. Ruskin, Sir Thomas Browne, and the *Revelations*. . . . My companions: hills, sir, and the sundown, and a dog as large as myself that my father bought me. They are better than kings, because they know, but do not tell.". . .

Six years later, when her nature was flowering under the sunshine of his appreciation, and the pruning of his criticism, she wrote to him—her "master": "Of our greatest acts we are ignorant. You were not aware that you saved my life. To thank you in person has been since then one of my few requests."

This was granted, and in 1870 occurred Higginson's first interview with the poet. She met her own description: "Small like the wren; and my hair is bold, like the chestnut burr; and my eyes like the sherry in the glass that the guest leaves." Another friend has said of her: "She was not beautiful, yet had many beauties"—a word that suits, too, her intellect.

I have not dwelt upon Emily Dickinson's faults; they speak for themselves, and sometimes with such a din that the virtues cannot be heard. Granted that her poetry is uneven, so rugged of rhyme and rhythm that it jolts the mind like a corduroy road—I prefer it to a flowery bed of ease. Many can lull, but few can awake.

Emily Dickinson's Puritan Heritage

John Robinson

Emily Dickinson's poems seem to exist outside of a historical context, refusing to answer such questions as Why here? and Why now? John Robinson, author of the study *Emily Dickinson: Looking to Canaan*, attempts to answer for her by locating the poet in her native New England town, in a different time— the time of the Salem witch trials.

In this new context, he proposes that Dickinson's reaction to the hysteria of the 1690s would likely be similar to her reaction to the American Civil War, which, although it was certainly the obsession of her time, hardly enters her poetry at all. He suggests to readers that her focus on what was timeless would not have allowed her to be blindly overtaken by any cause that she herself could not scrutinize honestly and carefully. To further his point, Robinson analyzes one short stanza that reveals much about Dickinson's view of time and history and compares his findings with those of previous critics.

'Tell it slant,' Emily Dickinson once advised. I want to begin, not with the nineteenth-century Amherst, Massachusetts, where she was born, but—though still in New England— some miles and years away in seventeenth-century Salem.

Notoriously, in 1692 her Puritan forebears were hanging witches there. Curious to know the future, young girls had made means to find out, amongst other things, about their likely marriages. The signs that they saw in the process frightened them and, in turn, their own disturbed behaviour alarmed their families who quickly regarded them as victims. Accusations were made. Trials were held. Enemies were executed.

From *Looking to Canaan* by John Robinson. Copyright 1986 by John Robinson. Reprinted by permission of the publisher, Faber & Faber, Ltd.

But there were still more accusations, more trials, more executions, till the judicial process itself seemed to be out of control. Piercing glances, touches, tetchiness might be interpreted as the public signs of private connection with malign power—and the interpretation might be lethal. There was judgement in the eye of the beholder and, however reluctant they might be to convict on 'spectral testimony', the tendency of the courts was to make the insubstantial real. Fear and mistrust produced their own map of what, in reflections published the following year, the Reverend Cotton Mather called *The Wonders of the Invisible World.*

History was being made out of belief; and those crucial, investigative questions, why *now*? why *here*?, were not allowed their proper weight. History was accounted for in terms which left time and place out of the reckoning. There was an incompleteness in the human response, a failure of intelligence which was scarcely distinguishable from a failure of that confidence which we call love.

It is hardly likely that Emily Dickinson would have been guilty of such failure. So lightly ironic was she about received opinion, so independent of the rigidities of dogma, that it is difficult to see her being possessed by the destructive vigour of the judges of Salem. She was not so narrowly purposeful, yet her inheritance was that tradition which celebrated the timeless wonders of the invisible world, and, in manifold ways, she, too, tended to lock history out of her imagination. An obvious example is that, although there are soldiers, battlefields, and martial imagery in her poems, the American Civil War, which came in the middle of her life, is missing from them. More generally, many of her poems resist the reader's enquiries about the where and when of location, and so resist, too, the attendant why here? and why now? which are part of the attempt to form a judgement. She does not help us to see how she might have changed or developed as a poet. Her poems are often reluctant to locate us in the circumstances of their generation. . . .

If we turn from the historians' Salem to Emily Dickinson we can see in the following slight stanza the ways in which her interest in timelessness is intimately connected with, effectively, a withdrawal from participation and a submission to the control of circumstances.

Witchcraft was hung, in History,
But History and I

Find all the Witchcraft that we need
Around us, every Day—

When? Where? Out of what process, and with what conse-
quences? Her mind does not work with such questions, so
time is telescoped and made inaccessible to us as 'in History'.
(There is no special significance in her capitals; generally
she used them, as in German, for nouns.) It is possible to
hang only witches, not witchcraft, so the first line is figurative and it is this figurativeness which facilitates one of the
two slippages in the poem. When it first appears 'witchcraft'
means the malefic working of pins stuck into poppets, of cer-
emonies to deploy the powers of darkness to cause suffering
or death; but 'Witchcraft' in the third line means the magic
of the wonderful, the marvellous, the extraordinary, the be-
nign. The poem turns on this pun. The other slippage is from
'History' meaning 'what is over and done with' to 'History'
meaning 'the sum of all pasts, presents and futures'. The
whole poem pivots on 'But': 'Witchcraft' is supposed to have
survived the assault made on it in the past and 'History' to be
truly shaped by what is innate in nature and not by something done long ago, once upon a time. We can have History
without historical events. History does not change: around
us, 'every Day', there is always 'Witchcraft'.

This stanza is one of those bright notes where she writes
with the air of someone who has pulled out a plum, and in
this it is not at all representative of her great poetry; but the
position she takes in it is characteristic of her thought and
indicates one of the reasons that some of her poems are difficult of approach. She wants to make human process (here,
of hanging in the past but not hanging now) unimportant
and a misperception. The witchcraft that is 'Around us,
every Day' is so persistent and undefined that it would obviously be futile to try to do anything to it. It is beyond human
power. Although its source is not located for us in the poem,
plainly it is not witches. In the past there was (repellent)
hanging, whereas there is now desirable magic. But the opposition in the poem is not really between now and then; it
is between then and always. It is not that we now know better, having learned from experience. It is that the past provides clear evidence of the way that human history is super-
fluous and in contrast there is another sort of history which
is real. The Olympian manner of 'History and I' marks not
transcendental arrogance but her sense of the secondariness

and the foreignness and the inertness of time when measured against the things which really matter.

What is this History which is untouched by history and which is the same every day?

DICKINSON IN THE PRESENT DAY

Emily Dickinson spent her life seeking to live in its dimensions—though she used other names and frames for it than the one in the poem above ('history' is a rare word in her vocabulary). It is as though she came to a conviction about the way her life should be oriented and then began to explore the implications of that orientation. Her thought was not progressive. It was not nourished by and dependent on thoughts that she had had before. In this sense it stayed still to dilate the moment and [*Looking to Canaan*] follows her in this by tracing her work not as a development but as an amplification. She had no project for her work. She did not carry through a purpose.

The effect of this has been to make her poems seem more than usually subject to the contingencies of circumstance—a chance meeting with a snake, or a hummingbird, a storm, some thoughts on a sunset. But when those poems are of great depth and turbulence and when, repeatedly, they revert to the same areas of disturbance, they encourage the view that there is an essential biographical pattern. Often commentators have felt that there is a story here if only they could find it, a novel of her life which would give them the generative springs.

Others have been less sanguine. She left behind nearly eighteen hundred lyrics—too many and too varied to be taken whole, and, though a tribute to the nomadic movement of her imagination, very uneven. Sometimes her poems are stringent, taut, fiercely alert; sometimes they are sentimental. Some show depths of insight and subtlety which set a reader's expectations high only for them to be betrayed by other work which, though it uses the same form and may set similar difficulties of approach, covers over the commonplace. Sometimes her tone is ironic, sometimes wistful; sometimes it is clamorous, sometimes plaintive, sometimes fulsome.

Faced with such multiplicity, R.P. Blackmur resorted to the desperate expedient of patronizing her thus:

She was a private poet who wrote indefatigably as some

women cook or knit. Her gift for words and the cultural predicament of her time drove her to poetry instead of anti-macassars.

This is to make her a poet of scraps, some of which are accidentally brilliant; but Adrienne Rich is struggling with the same essential difficulty when she says that Emily Dickinson was many poets, and so is David Porter in his campaigning: 'We find, no matter with what ingenuity we look, no solar system into whose gravitational field all her experiences were attracted.' Given the challenge of her multiplicity, we can see why Allen Tate's view that she was caught up in Emerson's war on Calvin has proved so durable. When we have an individual poet whose own work seems to fragment, an analogical claim is very persuasive. (R.P. Blackmur scoffed at him: 'When he has got his image all made he proceeds to sort out its component parts.')

It is apparent that we have to cope with a number of absences. Emily Dickinson is open to the making of theses because she never prepared her poems for publication, and to this editorial absence must be added the ambiguity and tentativeness of the dashes which she generally used in preference to firmer, conventional punctuation, and the lack of guidance which results from her poems being untitled. Nor did she leave, in either letter or essay, any extended prose discussion of the way she thought about her art. We are denied even secure texts or an unshakeable order of composition, and the man who has done most to give them to us observes of her poems: 'The dating of them is conjectural and for the most part will always remain so.'

The consequence is that inconvenient poems—there may be a number, for one mood contradicts another—may be neglected because any study of her work must necessarily be so very selective. Yet a piece of little merit on its own may receive much prominence because it illuminates some aspect of her thought, whereas a wonderful poem may be stubborn enough and opaque enough and so concentratedly itself as to make a reader doubt the illumination after all. We feel we need some secure centre which will enable us to determine what counts, and that seems to take us back to the story of her life.

I do not think that we should entirely relinquish this sense just because we cannot satisfy our curiosity. So figurative is Emily Dickinson's thought and so attracted by the riddle and the parable that it is difficult to believe that knowledge of, for example, the configurations of a frustrated love affair would not modify the contexts of some poems. So from her life-story we might receive significant help.

However, I think that underlying the biographical hope there has been a wish to provide what the verse does not provide and thus subtly to change its character by supplying its absences. We have little difficulty with time and place when she is writing about nature. The problems come with the space and span of poems which evoke states of feeling. We want to bring them under control by containing them under causes, yet I think that this shows an—understand-able—reluctance to cross their imaginative threshold and occupy them on their own terms. It is as if we wanted to think of the poems themselves as acts of management and to derive some control-system from them.

We can see that our own acts of naming are acts of man-agement which are achieved at the cost of severance. We refer, for example, to cedars, streams, birds' eggs and cloud formations as 'nature' and exclude from that word any pos-sible reference to smoke-stacks. But why should we divide the world so as to form a grouping which will bring together worms and sunshine, or connect the rainbow and the scor-pion? The word 'nature' makes a choice for us. In doing this it both releases and inhibits by giving us the resources but also putting on us the limitations of certain inherited ways of dividing up our experience with words. If we see Emily Dickinson as a poet of revelations we can see that in some sense she must be a poet of those moments when the words run out. Her very practice is a contradiction: using words to evoke the wordless, using words made in history to point be-yond history. If we see words as names and names as forms of control we can see that she is at a difficult intersection. . . .

In approaching her work we face, then, the contradiction that few have been less interested in temporal circumstances than she and that, at her finest, she prized those nameless moments when she seemed, with awe, to be at the edge of the eternal, yet we know about them only because she en-tered history, used the communal language, and was not simply a receptor but one who took initiatives as a creator. The kind of retreat we have from agency in the passive 'was hanged' of her witchcraft stanza sometimes carries through to the extent of her using uninflected verbs as if she could make an art of the infinitive. 'Be seen', 'arise', 'remit' are examples (from 'Further in Summer than the Birds'). In context are they past, present, or future? Are they first, second, or third person? They seem to wish to escape from time. Yet she could not. We have her work because of a series of interventions in history of which hers was the first and to which, in selecting and appraising as readers, we add another.

Emily Dickinson Ranks Among the World's Greatest Poets

Allen Tate

Author of numerous books of poetry, Allen Tate is perhaps best known for his poem "Ode to the Confederate Dead." His novel *The Fathers* was first published in 1928. Distinguished also as a critic, his collections of essays include *Reactionary Essays on Poetry and Ideas* and *Reason and Madness*. Tate was editor of such literary journals as the *Sewanee Review* and *Hound and Horn*. In this much-anthologized essay, Tate puts Dickinson in the company of the most famous poets of the Western world—John Donne, Alfred, Lord Tennyson, and William Shakespeare.

Personal revelation of the kind that [poets John] Donne and [Emily] Dickinson strove for, in the effort to understand their relation to the world, is a feature of all great poetry; it is probably the hidden motive for writing. It is the effort of the individual to live apart from a cultural tradition that no longer sustains him. But this culture, which I now wish to discuss a little, is indispensable: there is a great deal of shallow nonsense in modern criticism which holds that poetry—and this is a half-truth that is worse than false—is essentially revolutionary. It is only indirectly revolutionary: the intellectual and religious background of an age no longer contains the whole spirit, and the poet proceeds to examine that background in terms of immediate experience. But the background is necessary: otherwise all the arts (not only poetry) would have to rise in a vacuum. Poetry does not dispense with tradition; it probes the deficiencies of a tradition. But it must have a tradition to probe. It is too bad that [poet and critic Matthew] Arnold did not explain his doctrine, that poetry is a criticism of life, from the viewpoint of its back-

From "Emily Dickinson," in *Reactionary Essays on Poetry and Ideas* by Allen Tate (New York: Scribner, 1936). Reprinted by permission of Mrs. Allen Tate.

ground: we should have been spared an era of academic misconception, in which criticism of life meant a diluted pragmatism, the criterion of which was respectability. The poet in the true sense "criticizes" his tradition, either as such, or indirectly by comparing it with something that is about to replace it; he does what the root-meaning of the verb implies—he *discerns* its real elements and thus establishes its value, by putting it to the test of experience.

What is the nature of a poet's culture? Or, to put the question properly, what is the meaning of culture for poetry? All the great poets become the material of what we popularly call culture: we study them to acquire it. It is clear that [Joseph] Addison was more cultivated than [William] Shakespeare; nevertheless Shakespeare is a finer source of culture than Addison. What is the meaning of this? Plainly it is that learning has never had anything to do with culture except instrumentally: the poet must be exactly literate enough to write down fully and precisely what he has to say, but no more. The source of a poet's true culture lies back of the paraphernalia of culture, and not all the historical activity of an enlightened age can create it.

A culture cannot be consciously created. It is an available source of ideas that are imbedded in a complete and homogeneous society. The poet finds himself balanced upon the moment when such a world is about to fall, when it threatens to run out into looser and less self-sufficient impulses. This world order is assimilated, in Miss Dickinson, as medievalism was in Shakespeare, to the poetic vision; it is brought down from abstraction to personal sensibility.

BETWEEN THOUGHT AND FEELING

In this connection it may be said that the prior conditions for great poetry, given a great talent, may be reduced to two: the thoroughness of the poet's discipline in an objective system of truth, and his lack of consciousness of such a discipline. For this discipline is a number of fundamental ideas the origin of which the poet does not know; they give form and stability to his fresh perceptions of the world; and he cannot shake them off. This is his culture, and, like Tennyson's God, it is nearer than hands and feet. With reasonable certainty we unearth the elements of Shakespeare's culture, and yet it is equally certain—so innocent was he of his own resources— that he would not know what our discussion is about. He appeared at the collapse of the medieval system as a rigid pattern of life, but that pattern remained in Shakespeare what Shelley called a "fixed point of reference" for his sensibility. Miss Dickinson, as we have seen, was born into the equilibrium of an old and a new order. Puritanism could not be to her what it had been to the generation of Cotton Mather—a body of absolute truths: it was an unconscious discipline timed to the pulse of her life.

TO EMILY DICKINSON

Hart Crane was one of many poets of substance to be profoundly influenced by the work of Emily Dickinson. In this poem, from his Complete Poems and Selected Letters, *Crane laments the fact that Dickinson was fully appreciated only after her death.*

You who desired so much—in vain to ask—
Yet fed your hunger like an endless task,
Dared dignify the labor, bless the quest—
Achieved that stillness ultimately best,

Being, of all, least sought for: Emily, hear!
O sweet, dead Silencer, most suddenly clear
When singing that Eternity possessed
And plundered momently in every breast;

—Truly no flower yet withers in your hand,
The harvest you descried and understand
Needs more than wit to gather, love to bind.
Some reconcilement of remotest mind—

Leaves Ormus rubyless, and Ophir chill.
Else tears heap all within one clay-cold hill.

The perfect literary situation: it produces, because it is rare, a special and perhaps the most distinguished kind of poet. I am not trying to invent a new critical category. Such poets are never very much alike on the surface; they show us all the varieties of poetic feeling; and, like other poets, they resist all classification but that of temporary convenience. But, I believe, Miss Dickinson and John Donne would have this in common: their sense of the natural world is not blunted by a too-rigid system of ideas: yet the ideas, the abstractions, their education or their intellectual heritage, are not so weak as to let their immersion in nature, or their purely personal quality, get out of control. The two poles of the mind are not separately visible; we infer them from the lucid tension that may be most readily illustrated by polar activity. There is no thought as such at all: nor is there feeling: there is that unique focus of experience which is at once neither and both.

Like Miss Dickinson, Shakespeare is without opinions: his peculiar merit is also deeply involved in his failure to think about anything; his meaning is not in the content of his expression: it is in the tension of the dramatic relations of his characters. This kind of poetry is at the opposite of intellectualism. (Miss Dickinson is obscure and difficult, but that is not intellectualism.) To T.W. Higginson, the editor of the *Atlantic Monthly*, who tried to advise her, she wrote that she had no education. In any sense that Higginson could understand, it was quite true. His kind of education was the conscious cultivation of abstractions. She did not reason about the world she saw: she merely saw it. The "ideas" implicit in the world within her rose up, concentrated in her immediate perception.

That kind of world at present has for us something of the fascination of a buried city. There is none like it. When such worlds exist, when such cultures flourish, they support not only the poet but all members of society. For, from these, the poet differs only in his gift for exhibiting the structure, the internal lineaments, of his culture by threatening to tear them apart: a process that concentrates the symbolic emotions of society while it seems to attack them. The poet may hate his age; he may be an outcast like Villon; but this world is always there as the background to what he has to say. It is the lens through which he brings nature to focus and control—the clarifying medium that concentrates his personal feeling. It is ready-made; he cannot make it; with it, his poetry has a spontaneity and a certainty of direction that, without it, it would lack. No poet could have invented the ideas of "The Chariot," only a great poet could have found their imaginative equivalents. Miss Dickinson was a deep mind writing from a deep culture, and when she came to poetry, she came infallibly.

DICKINSON'S CRITICISM DESERVES ATTENTION

Infallibly, at her best; for no poet has ever been perfect, nor is Emily Dickinson. Her precision of statement is due to the directness with which the abstract framework of her thought acts upon its unorganized material. The two elements of her style, considered as point of view, are immortality, or the idea of permanence, and the physical process of death or decay. Her diction has two corresponding features: words of Latin or Greek origin and, sharply opposed to these, the concrete Saxon element. It is this verbal conflict that gives her verse its high tension; it is not a device deliberately seized upon, but a feeling for language that senses out the two fundamental components of English and their metaphysical relation: the Latin for ideas and the Saxon for perceptions—the peculiar virtue of English as a poetic language.

Like most poets Miss Dickinson often writes out of habit: the style that emerged from some deep exploration of an idea is carried on as verbal habit when she has nothing to say. She indulges herself:

> There's something quieter than sleep
> Within this inner room!
> It wears a sprig upon its breast,
> And will not tell its name.
>
> Some touch it and some kiss it,
> Some chafe its idle hand:
> It has a simple gravity
> I do not understand!
>
> While simple hearted neighbors
> Chat of the "early dead,"
> We, prone to periphrasis,
> Remark that birds have fled!

It is only a pert remark; at best a superior kind of punning—one of the worst specimens of her occasional interest in herself. But she never had the slightest interest in the public. Were four poems or five published in her lifetime? She never felt the temptation to round off a poem for public exhibition. Higginson's kindly offer to make her verse "correct" was an invitation to throw her work into the public ring—the ring of Lowell and Longfellow. He could not see that he was tampering with one of the rarest literary integrities of all time. Here was a poet who had no use for the supports of authorship—flattery and fame; she never needed money.

She had all the elements of a culture that has broken up, a culture that on the religious side takes its place in the museum of spiritual antiquities. Puritanism, as a unified version of the world, is dead; only a remnant of it in trade may be said to survive. In the history of puritanism she comes between Hawthorne and Emerson. She has Hawthorne's matter, which a too irresponsible personality tends to dilute into a form like Emerson's; she is often betrayed by words. But she is not the poet of personal sentiment; she has more to say than she can put down in any one poem. Like Hardy and Whitman, she must be read entire; like Shakespeare, she never gives up her meaning in a single line.

She is therefore a perfect subject for the kind of criticism which is chiefly concerned with general ideas. She exhibits one of the permanent relations between personality and objective truth, and she deserves the special attention of our time, which lacks that kind of truth.

She has Hawthorne's intellectual toughness, a hard, definite sense of the physical world. The highest flights to God, the most extravagant metaphors of the strange and the remote, come back to a point of casuistry, to a moral dilemma of the experienced world. There is, in spite of the homiletic vein of utterance, no abstract speculation, nor is there a message to society; she speaks wholly to the individual experience. She offers to the unimaginative no riot of vicarious sensation; she has no useful maxims for men of action. Up to this point her resemblance to Emerson is slight: poetry is a sufficient form of utterance, and her devotion to it is pure. But in Emily Dickinson the puritan world is no longer self-contained; it is no longer complete; her sensibility exceeds its dimensions. She has trimmed down its supernatural proportions; it has become a morality; instead of the tragedy of the spirit there is a commentary upon it. Her poetry is a magnificent personal confession, blasphemous and, in its self-revelation, its honesty, almost obscene. It comes out of an intellectual life toward which it feels no moral responsibility. Cotton Mather would have burnt her for a witch.

CHAPTER 2

Poetic Analysis

READINGS ON

EMILY DICKINSON

Two Explications

Nancy Lenz Harvey and Thomas H. Johnson

An explication is a line-by-line prose interpretation of a poem. Because poetry often employs such techniques as word ambiguity, paradox, and compression, explication is usually much less simple than it would appear by definition. Similarly, the explication itself is open to interpretive readings since the way a reader views a text has everything to do with education, associations, and personal biases.

What follows are two of Dickinson's poems as they are explicated by some of the finest scholars in the field. The first explication, Nancy Lenz Harvey's "What Soft Cherubic Creatures," appeared in a 1969–1970 volume of the *Explicator*, a journal devoted to poetic interpretation. The second explication is from Thomas H. Johnson's book-length study *Emily Dickinson: An Interpretive Biography*, first published in 1955.

"WHAT SOFT CHERUBIC CREATURES"

What Soft—Cherubic Creatures—
These Gentlewomen are—
One would as soon assault a Plush—
Or violate a Star—

Such Dimity Convictions—
A Horror so refined
Of freckled Human Nature—
Of Deity—ashamed—

It's such a common—Glory—
A Fisherman's—Degree—
Redemption—Brittle Lady—
Be so—ashamed of Thee—

Emily Dickinson's "What Soft Cherubic Creatures" is a sting-

Part I, Nancy Lenz Harvey, "Dickinson's 'What Soft Cherubic Creatures,'" *Explicator*, vol. 28 (1970). Reprinted with permission of the Helen Dwight Reid Educational Foundation. Published by Heldref Publications, 1319 18th St. NW, Washington, DC 20036-1802. Copyright ©1970. Part II, from *Emily Dickinson: An Interpretive Biography* by Thomas H. Johnson (Cambridge, MA: Harvard University Press); ©1955 by the President and Fellows of Harvard College. Reprinted by permission of the publisher.

ing denunciation of the hypocrisy embodied in gentlewomen. Although they appear delicate and remote—"One would as soon assault a Plush / Or violate a Star" (lines 3-4)—these ladies are neither soft nor cherubic. Their very label is a misnomer; their invective against humankind and the Godhead is anything but gentle. This first stanza is then both caustic and satirical.

BEAUTY LIES IN HUMAN IMPERFECTIONS

The second stanza explicates reasons for the poet's tone. These ladies with their dainty, delicate, "dimity" convictions and their "refined" horror are abashed by "freckled Human Nature" (lines 5-7). Human nature, besmirched by original sin, contains within it all the *ugliness* of the flesh, sin and sex—ideas abhorrent to the *gentler* sort. Yet as the ladies shame the flesh, they inadvertently shame the Deity, for man is made in God's image.

These first two stanzas seem to be clear and straightforward, while the third and final stanza becomes curiously ambiguous, and the punctuation of stanzas 2 and 3 increases this ambiguity. If the lines "It's such a common—glory— / A Fisherman's—Degree—" (lines 9-10) are read as part of those "Dimity Convictions," the flesh is condemned once more because it is a *common* glory—a second-rate glory. It is thus of low estate, that level of society known only to the laborer, the "fisherman's degree." The words *common* and *degree* are often spouted by those who feel themselves remote from the herd, who fail to see a humanity basic to all men.

If, however, these lines begin another thought, then the poem moves progressively to a theological note, and the diction—"common glory," "fisherman's degree," and "redemption"—reinforces this note. Not only are the ladies in horror of human nature, made in the image of God, but they have also failed to realize that human nature is the common or shared glory of God and man. This is the nature chosen by God as He becomes the man Jesus— the man who is a fisher of men. Since the purpose of Christ's life and passion is solely for the redemption of human nature, the closing lines are closely related to the poem as a whole. The ladies are now rightly called: they are "brittle" ladies capable of meanness and sharp cruelty; for they have not only denied the humanity of others and of themselves, but they have also denied their God. Redemption, if now, would "be ashamed" of them.

The rich ambiguity of this last stanza tightens the unity of the poem. The theological reading strengthens the tie of the last two lines to the poem as a whole and combines with the other reading to underscore the superciliousness of the ladies. The cherubic ladies of the opening line become nothing less than alienated creatures who have so distanced themselves from both God and man that they are more *mineral* than *human*—they are brittle creatures. . . .

"Because I Could Not Stop for Death"

In 1863 Death came into full stature as a person. "Because I could not stop for Death" is a superlative achievement wherein Death becomes one of the great characters of literature.

It is almost impossible in any critique to define exactly the kind of reality which her character Death attains, simply because the protean shifts of form are intended to forestall definition. A poem can convey the nuances of exultation, agony, compassion, or any mystical mood. But no one can successfully define mysticism because the logic of language has no place for it. One must therefore assume that the reality of Death, as Emily Dickinson conceived him, is to be perceived by the reader in the poems themselves. Any analysis can do no more than suggest what may be looked for.

In "Because I could not stop for Death" Emily Dickinson envisions Death as a person she knew and trusted, or believed that she could trust. He might be any Amherst gentleman . . . who at one time or another had acted as her squire.

> Because I could not stop for Death—
> He kindly stopped for me—
> The Carriage held but just Ourselves—
> And Immortality.

The carriage holds but the two of them, yet the ride, as she states with quiet emphasis, is a last ride together. Clearly there has been no deception on his part. They drive in a leisurely manner, and she feels completely at ease. Since she understands it to be a last ride, she of course expects it to be unhurried. Indeed, his graciousness in taking time to stop for her at that point and on that day in her life when she was so busy she could not possibly have taken time to stop for him, is a mark of special politeness. She is therefore quite willing to put aside her work. And again, since it is to be her last ride, she can dispense with her spare moments as well as her active ones.

> We slowly drove—He knew no haste
> And I had put away
> My labor and my leisure too
> For His Civility—

She notes the daily routine of the life she is passing from. Children playing games during a school recess catch her eye at the last. And now the sense of motion is quickened. Or perhaps more exactly one should say that the sense of time comes to an end as they pass the cycles of the day and the seasons of the year, at a period of both ripeness and decline.

> We passed the School, where Children strove
> At Recess—in the Ring—
> We passed the Fields of Gazing Grain—
> We passed the Setting Sun—

How insistently "passed" echoes through the stanza! She now conveys her feeling of being outside time and change, for she corrects herself to say that the sun passed them, as it of course does all who are in the grave. She is aware of dampness and cold, and becomes suddenly conscious of the sheerness of the dress and scarf which she now discovers that she wears.

> Or rather—He passed Us—
> The Dews drew quivering and chill—
> For only Gossamer, my Gown—
> My Tippet—only Tulle—

The two concluding stanzas, with progressively decreasing concreteness, hasten the final identification of her "House." It is the slightly rounded surface "of the Ground," with a scarcely visible roof and a cornice "in the Ground." To time and seasonal change, which have already ceased, is now added motion. Cessation of all activity and creativeness is absolute. At the end, in a final instantaneous flash of memory, she recalls the last objects before her eyes during the journey: the heads of the horses that bore her, as she had surmised they were doing from the beginning, toward—it is the last word—"Eternity."

> We paused before a House that seemed
> A Swelling of the Ground—
> The Roof was scarcely visible—
> The Cornice—in the Ground—
>
> Since then—'tis Centuries—and yet
> Feels shorter than the Day
> I first surmised the Horses Heads
> Were toward Eternity—

Gradually, too, one realizes that Death as a person has receded into the background, mentioned last only impersonally in the opening words "We paused" of the fifth stanza, where his services as squire and companion are over. In this poem concrete realism melds into "awe and circumference" with matchless economy.

Diverging Viewpoints on a Classic Poem

Gerhard Friedrich, John Ciardi, and Caroline Hogue

Three critics discuss one of Dickinson's most popular poems, "I Heard a Fly buzz—when I died—." The discussion begins with an analysis by Gerhard Friedrich which appeared in the *Explicator*—a scholarly journal devoted entirely to interpreting single poems—in 1955. In this essay, Friedrich states that to understand this much-discussed poem, a reader first needs to answer two questions: What is the significance of the fly buzzing? and what does the repetition of the word *see* in the last line mean?

While Friedrich's response to the second question seems to have stirred little controversy, his answers to the first drew a quick reaction from John Ciardi in the *Explicator* some months later. Then in 1961, Caroline Hogue responded to Ciardi's analysis by offering some historical facts that contradict both critics' interpretations. It is interesting to note that Ciardi was no longer sure he agreed with all he said in his essay, although he remained convinced of his main point.

I heard a Fly buzz—when I died—
The Stillness in the Room
Was like the Stillness in the Air—
Between the Heaves of Storm—

The Eyes around—had wrung them dry—
And Breaths were gathering firm
For that last Onset—when the King
Be witnessed—in the Room—

I willed my Keepsakes—Signed away
What portion of me be
Assignable—and then it was
There interposed a Fly—

Gerhard Friedrich, "Dickinson's 'I Heard a Fly Buzz When I Died,'" *Explicator*, vol. 13, April 1955; John Ciardi, a response to Friedrich in the January 1956 issue of the *Explicator*, and Caroline Hogue's response to both Friedrich and Ciardi in the November 1961 *Explicator*. Reprinted with permission of the Helen Dwight Reid Educational Foundation. Published by Heldref Publications, 1319 18th St. NW, Washington, DC 20036-1802; ©1955, 1956, 1961.

With Blue—uncertain stumbling Buzz—
Between the light—and me—
And then the Windows failed—and then
I could not see to see—
                    (#465)

GERHARD FRIEDRICH

This poem seems to present two major problems to the in-
terpreter. First, what is the significance of the buzzing fly in
relation to the dying person, and second, what is the meaning of the double use of "see" in the last line? An analysis of
the context helps to clear up these apparent obscurities, and
a close parallel found in another Dickinson poem reinforces
such interpretation.

In an atmosphere of outward quiet and inner calm, the
dying person collectedly proceeds to bequeath his or her
worldly possessions, and while engaged in this activity of
"willing," finds his attention withdrawn by a fly's buzzing.
The fly is introduced in intimate connection with "my keepsakes" and "what portion of me be assignable"; it follows—
and is the culmination of—the dying person's preoccupation
with cherished material things no longer of use to the departing owner. In the face of death, and even more of a possible spiritual life beyond death, one's concern with a few
earthly belongings is but a triviality, and indeed a distraction
from a momentous issue. The obtrusiveness of the inferior,
physical aspects of existence, and the busybody activity associated with them, is poignantly illustrated by the interven-
ing insect (cf. the line "Buzz the dull flies on the chamber
window," in the poem beginning "How many times these
low feet staggered"). Even so small a demonstrative, demonstrable creature is sufficient to separate the dying person
from "the light," i.e. to blur the vision, to short-circuit mental concentration, so that spiritual awareness is lost. The last
line of the poem may then be paraphrased to read: "Waylaid
by irrelevant, tangible, finite objects of little importance, I
was no longer capable of that deeper perception which
would clearly reveal to me the infinite spiritual reality." As
Emily Dickinson herself expressed it, in another Second Series poem beginning "Their height in heaven comforts not":

I'm finite, I can't see.
            .   .   .   .
This timid life of evidence
Keeps pleading, "I don't know."

The dying person does in fact not merely suffer an unwelcome external interruption of an otherwise resolute expectancy, but falls from a higher consciousness, from liberating insight, from faith, into an intensely skeptical mood. The fly's buzz is characterized as "blue, uncertain, stumbling," and emphasis on the finite physical reality goes hand in hand with a frustrating lack of absolute assurance. The only portion of a man not properly "assignable" may be that which dies and decomposes! To the dying person, the buzzing fly would thus become a timely, untimely reminder of man's final, cadaverous condition and putrefaction.

The sudden fall of the dying person into the captivity of an earth-heavy skepticism demonstrates of course the inadequacy of the earlier pseudo-stoicism. What seemed then like composure, was after all only a pause "between the heaves of storm"; the "firmness" of the second stanza proved to be less than veritable peace of mind and soul; and so we have a profoundly tragic human situation, namely the perennial conflict between two concepts of reality, most carefully delineated.

The poem should be compared with its illuminating counterpart of the Second Series, "Their height in heaven comforts not," and may be contrasted with "Death is a dialogue between," "I heard as if I had no ear," and the well-known "I never saw a moor."

JOHN CIARDI

I read Mr. Gerhard Friedrich's explication . . . of Emily Dickinson's poem with great interest, but I find myself preferring a different explication.

Mr. Friedrich says of the fly: "Even so small a demonstrative, demonstrable creature is sufficient to separate the dying person from 'the light,' i.e. to blur the vision, to short-circuit mental concentration, so that spiritual awareness is lost. The last line of the poem may then be paraphrased to read: 'Waylaid by irrelevant, tangible, finite objects of little importance, I was no longer capable of that deeper perception which would clearly reveal to me the infinite spiritual reality.'"

Mr. Friedrich's argument is coherent and respectable, but I feel it tends to make Emily more purely mystical than I sense her to be. I understand that fly to be the last kiss of the world, the last buzz from life. Certainly Emily's tremendous attachment to the physical world, and her especial delight both in minute creatures for their own sake, and in minute actions for the sake of the dramatic implications that can be loaded into them, hardly needs to be documented. Any number of poems illustrate her delight in the special significance of tiny living things. "Elysium is as Far" will do as a single example of her delight in packing a total-life significance into the slightest actions:

> What fortitude the Soul contains,
> That it can so endure
> The accent of a coming Foot—
> The opening of a Door—

I find myself better persuaded, therefore, to think of the fly not as a distraction taking Emily's thoughts from glory and blocking the divine light (When did Emily ever think of living things as a distraction?), but as a last dear sound from the world as the light of consciousness sank from her, i.e. "the windows failed." And so I take the last line to mean simply: "And then there was no more of me, and nothing to see with."

In writing her best poems [Emily Dickinson] was never at the mercy of her emotions or of the official rhetoric. She mastered her themes by controlling her language. She could achieve a novel significance, for example, by starting with a death scene that implies the orthodox questions and then turning the meaning against itself by the strategy of surprise answers.... ["I heard a Fly buzz—when I died"] operates in terms of all the standard religious assumptions of her New England, but with a difference. They are explicitly gathered up in one phrase for the moment of death, with distinct Biblical overtones, "that last Onset—when the King / Be witnessed—in the Room." But how is he witnessed?

As the poet dramatizes herself in a deathbed scene, with family and friends gathered round, her heightened senses report the crisis in flat domestic terms that bring to the reader's mind each of the traditional questions only to deny them without even asking them. Her last words were squandered in distributing her "Keepsakes," trivial tokens of this life rather than messages from the other. The only sound of heavenly music, or of wings taking flight, was the "Blue— uncertain stumbling Buzz" of a fly that filled her dying ear. Instead of a final vision of the hereafter, this world simply faded from her eyes: the light in the windows failed and then she "could not see to see." The King witnessed in this power is physical death, not God. To take this poem literally as an attempted inside view of the gradual extinction of consciousness and the beginning of the soul's flight into eternity would be to distort its meaning, for this is not an imaginative projection of her own death. In structure, in language, in imagery it is simply an ironic reversal of the conventional attitudes of her time and place toward the significance of the moment of death. Yet mystery is evoked by a single word, that extraordinarily interposed color "Blue."

To misread such a poem would be to misunderstand the whole cast of Dickinson's mind. Few poets saw more clearly the boundary between what can and what cannot be comprehended, and so held the mind within its proper limitations. . . .

CAROLINE HOGUE

Emily Dickinson's "I Heard A Fly Buzz When I Died" should be read, I think, with a particular setting in mind—a nineteenth-century deathbed scene. Before the age of powerful anodynes death was met in full consciousness, and the way of meeting it tended to be stereotype. It was affected with a public interest and concern, and was witnessed by family and friends. They crowded the death chamber to await expectantly a burst of dying energy to bring on the grand act of passing. Commonly it began with last-minute bequests, the wayward were called to repentance, the back-slider to reform, gospel hymns were sung, and finally as climax the dying one gave witness in words to the Redeemer's presence in the room, how He hovered, transplendent in the upper air, with open arms outstretched to receive the departing soul. This was death's great moment. Variants there were, of course, in case of repentant and unrepentant sinners. Here in this poem the central figure of the drama is expected to make a glorious exit. The build-up is just right for it, but at the moment of climax "There interposed a fly." And what kind of a fly? A fly "with blue, uncertain stumbling buzz"—a blowfly.

How right is Mr. Gerhard Friedrich in his explication . . . to associate the fly with putrefaction and decay. And how wrong, I think, is Mr. John Ciardi . . . in calling the fly "the last kiss of the world," and speaking of it as one of the small creatures Emily Dickinson so delighted in. She could not possibly have entertained any such view of a blowfly. She was a practical housewife, and every housewife abhors a blowfly. It pollutes everything it touches. Its eggs are maggots. It is as carrion as a buzzard.

What we know of Emily Dickinson gives us assurance that just as she would abhor the blowfly she would abhor the deathbed scene. How devastatingly she disposes of the projected one in the poem. "They talk of hallowed things and embarrass my dog" she writes in 1862 in a letter to [her friend and mentor Thomas W.] Higginson.

An Explication of "The first Day's Night had come"

Constance Rooke

Canadian scholar Constance Rooke conducts a line-by-line examination of one of Dickinson's more complex poems. Rooke reveals meaning in the poem by analyzing such aspects as plot, tone, and metaphor and derives the multiple meanings that are evident in all good poems.

The first Day's Night had come—
And grateful that a thing
So terrible—had been endured—
I told my Soul to sing—

She said her Strings were snapt—
Her Bow—to Atoms blown—
And so to mend her—gave me work
Until another Morn—

And then—a Day as huge
As Yesterdays in pairs,
Unrolled its horror in my face—
Until it blocked my eyes—

My Brain—begun to laugh—
I mumbled—like a fool—
And tho' 'tis Years ago—that Day—
My Brain keeps giggling—still.

And Something's odd—within—
That person that I was—
And this One—do not feel the same—
Could it be Madness—this?
                    (#410)

"The first Day's Night had come" is a lyric projected as drama. Its time begins on the first day of the speaker's new life: a life wholly formed as the aftermath of "a thing / So terrible" that it has created a radical discontinuity in the life and

Constance Rooke, "'The First Day's Night Had Come': An Explication of J.410," *Emily Dickinson Bulletin*, vol. 24 (1973). Reprinted by permission of the author.

personality of its endurer. Characters are born within the speaker, characters whose job it is to piece out the future of pain in dialogue and protective, ironic gesture. The tone which arises in the poem is crucially ironic and naked at the same time; all disguises reveal, and are created by, the lacerated passions beneath. From this tension, if at all, the speaker must summon continuance and its doubtful blessing.

The poem begins:

> The first Day's Night had come—
> And grateful that a thing
> So terrible—had been endured—
> I told my Soul to sing—

We need not speculate on the identity of that thing so terrible, which almost inevitably presents itself to our imaginations as the loss of a lover, or a possible psychosis. With this first speech there are other questions more problematic. Is it likely that she should be grateful for only this brief and bare endurance? And out of what mood, given this situation, does one tell one's soul to sing? On the one hand, she may indeed be grateful, astonished that she has in any fashion survived so far. Then the injuction to her soul may be delirious and earnest. On the other hand, this talking to one's soul may be to begin a mad game. Souls, furthermore, do not ordinarily need to be commanded into song; they are supposed to do that spontaneously. Her gratitude may be a mocking of her own deprivation, and her order to the soul a grim recognition that free song is past.

> She said her Strings were snapt—
> Her bow—to Atoms blown—
> And so to mend her—gave me work
> Until another Morn—

The personified soul's reply extends the metaphor with unpleasant, deadly restraint. The metaphor is the poet's toy, her effort to stay despair. Within the terms of the metaphor, the soul-mending is similarly busy-work. One questions whether the soul were put together again by that next morning. It is a tidy little image for such an ultimate task, its limitations suggesting a patchwork job at best.

> And then—a Day as huge
> As Yesterdays in pairs,
> Unrolled its horror in my face—
> Until it blocked my eyes—

If she had thought her night work effective, she rose to find

it far otherwise. She had tried to manage her pain in minia-
ture compass, within the play world established between
herself and a doll soul. But daylight brought monstrous
twins to threaten the dollmaker. There is no possessive
apostrophe in "Yesterdays," which helps us to see the day in
pairs. Perhaps as malicious footmen, giants who unroll their
horror as if at the start of a carpet which will only be un-
wound at her life's end. Most of their horror is in the dupli-
cation of her pain; each day will it be twice as bad as the day
before? This horizontal nightmare leaves only the alternative of the barren, vertical self out of time. She is so appalled
by the vision of her anguished situation that her eyes are
blocked and she turns inward.

> My Brain—begun to laugh—
> I mumbled—like a fool—
> And tho' 'tis Years ago—that Day—
> My Brain keeps giggling—still.

Reality cannot be endured, but there is nowhere else to live.
In the vacuum, after the shock of withdrawal, laughter
sounds. It must be someone else who laughs so cruelly as if
to reveal the prison and the foolishness of struggle. The sick-
ened brain, bereft of intellectual power by this departure
from reality, diverges from the speaker to become a separate
character. Marvellous, covert syntax suggests this confusion
of identity. The speaker is reduced to mumbling in the face
of the brain's superior laughter; but she also "mumbled" the
brain to begin with, foolishly, and so created her own half-
witted tormentor. Thus, "like a fool" applies to both the
laughter and the mumbling, and ultimately to the schizo-
phrenic retreat which deprives her of reality and the faint
hope of renewal. Years later, the laughter has subsided to
giggles but the hideous joke persists. The extent of this defeat is queried in the final stanza.

> And Something's odd—within—
> That person that I was—
> And this One—do not feel the same—
> Could it be Madness—this?

"That person" is remote. The vague remarking of the fact
that "Something's odd—within," the pause before "—
within" like a fearful admission of her residence there or shy
pretense of a distinction no longer valid, suggest the seriousness of her discontinuity. And there is a childishness in
her expression of the sense that these two persons do not

feel the same. The speaker is docile now, fading out—as good a definition of madness, perhaps, as any. Certainly the reader's horror is greater here than in that other country where the speaker still wrestled with her demons.

Editorial Decisions Affect Dickinson Collections

Marta L. Werner

When Emily Dickinson died in 1886, she left behind several bound books, or "fascicles," that have since been published in various forms and under several titles. In addition to the fascicles she left many separate poems, scraps, and ideas behind, some completed, some in various states of development. It is impossible to know how Dickinson intended her work to be collected—if in fact she meant her work to be collected at all.

Essayist Marta L. Werner asserts that because any act of editing, including changing Dickinson's distinctive handwriting into typed letters, necessarily changes the way we read the poems, editing Dickinson's poems today "paradoxically involves unediting them." When we return the slashes, variant word choices, even the writing in the margins, we not only see intended messages more clearly, we see Dickinson as a forerunner to many postmodern writers who have just recently begun experimenting with unconventional methods of presentation similar to Dickinson's self-edited works. Werner is the author of *Emily Dickinson's Open Folios: Scenes of Reading, Surfaces of Writing*, from which this article is excerpted.

In 1858 or 1859 Emily Dickinson began binding her work into the small packets that her first editors, Mabel Loomis Todd and Thomas Wentworth Higginson, called *fascicles*: a cluster of flowers, the leaves of a book. To assemble a packet Dickinson first copied her poems in ink onto uniform sheets of stationery, then stacked several copied sheets together, stabbed two holes in the set, at last threading them through

From the Introduction to *Emily Dickinson's Open Folios: Scenes of Reading, Surfaces of Writing* by Marta L. Werner (Ann Arbor: University of Michigan Press, 1995). Copyright ©1995 by Marta L. Werner. Reprinted by permission of the author and publisher.

with string tied once in the front. In the earliest packets poems are fitted into blank spaces on the page, few alternate word choices appear to complicate readings, and ambiguities are neatly ~~struck out~~. Later, however, in the creatively charged 1860s, a significant change takes place inside of the fascicles, a change almost certainly reflecting a change in Dickinson's attitude toward "final authorial intention." At this juncture the packets take on the character of a workshop: variant word choices appear in abundance, and the almost habitual quatrain of the early work is ruptured and transformed under the pressures of a new vision.

In 1981 Ralph W. Franklin completed his vast facsimile edition of *The Manuscript Books of Emily Dickinson.* In his edition Franklin restores, as far as is currently possible, the original order and internal sequence of the forty fascicles, revises the dating schema of the [Thomas H.] Johnson variorum, and charts Dickinson's poetic activity up until approximately 1864, when she ceased attempts at fine, handcrafted bookmaking. The focus of Franklin's edition, then, is those poems that, though never authorized by Dickinson for circulation in the realm of public discourse, may be understood as [what Franklin calls in his introduction] "a personal enactment of the public act that, for reasons unexplained, she denied herself."

On the one hand, the immense erudition and scholarly authority of Franklin's edition confirm the gigantic authority of Dickinson's poetry. On the other hand, the source of Franklin's authority as editor of Dickinson's work may be fundamentally different, even antithetical, to the authority of the writing itself, and to Dickinson's art—her rigor—of "choosing not choosing." [To borrow the title of Sharon Cameron's book on Dickinson's fascicles.] By the very act of entering the loved work of an author into the social and economic networks of distribution, an editor necessarily chooses to choose; the creation of what Jonathan Arac calls an "authoritative critical identity" for Emily Dickinson requires that there be omissions and exclusions: *of* fragments, scraps, lost events. *The Manuscript Books of Emily Dickinson,* edited by Franklin in two volumes, offers a portrait of the artist as bookmaker: what is central—that is, canonical—is what was/is bound in a book.

Yet what if, as Cameron wonders, "Dickinson is looking for her own language and finding it in the margins"?

"SUNDAY—SECOND OF MARCH"

Leaving Dickinson's poems and fragments as close to the original as possible allows interpretations impossible under previous editors. This fragment, collected in Marta Werner's Open Folios, *was originally written in pencil, the left and right margins in a lighter hand. The date of the fragment is March 2, 1884.*

```
Of                 Sunday —

        Second      of      March
                                  /
        and     the     Crow
injury                       /            when
        and     Snow     high
                                          passed
        as      the      Spire
                                /
        and        scarlet              it
                                       passed
too   Expectations        of

        things    that    never

        come  |   because           know   it
innocent
        forever      here —
(( 
        The       Twilight    says

        to     the       Turret

        if     you       want

        an       Existence           To
```

Emily Dickinson did not stop writing in 1864; rather, she stopped writing *books*. In the final decade of her life, sometimes called the "late prolific period," Dickinson abandoned even the minimal bibliographical apparatus of the fascicles, along with their dialectical structure, to explore a language as free in practice as in theory and to induce the unbinding of the scriptural economy. "Strange," as Rilke wrote in *The*

Duino Elegies, "to see meanings that clung together once, floating away / in every direction." In the 1870s and 1880s the leaves of the folios lie scattered: the end of linearity is signaled not in their apparent disorder but, rather, in their apprehension of multiple or contingent orders. No longer marking a place in a book, the loose leaves of stationery and scraps of paper are risked to still wilder forms of circulation: "Joy and Gravitation have their own ways."

As Susan Howe and others have pointed out, the signs of a fundamental ambivalence toward synthesis and closure that culminated in the scattering of manuscript leaves in the last decade of Dickinson's life are present in her work almost from its inception. Around 1860 the first variant word lists appear along the fringes of Dickinson's poems like an alien voicing, disturbing set borders and summoning into the work [again quoting Cameron] the "spell of difference." Here "the desire for limit" gives way before "the difficulty in enforcing it." Thus, Emily Dickinson's manuscript books— and here I refer not to Franklin's twentieth-century reconstructions but to the packets themselves—define a boundary that is also a threshold at "the austere reach of the book." [See Susan Howe's *The Birth-mark.*] Beyond this threshold, itself an unstable one, lie the rough and fair copy drafts of poems composed after Dickinson ceased binding her work into volumes, the letters she wrote over the course of a lifetime, and, most problematically of all, a large number of extrageneric materials—now generally labeled prose fragments and drafts—written after 1870 and left in various stages of composition and crisis at the time of her death. These writings belong to a forgotten canon. . . .

There can never be an authorized edition of Dickinson's writings. The gold imprimatur—emblem or face of Harvard's authority stamped across the blue binding of Johnson's *Letters* (1958)—is a false witness: like displaced enunciations, the drafts and fragments escape from the plot of "pure scholarship" to reappear always outside the *texte propre* and the law of the censor. . . . Today editing Emily Dickinson's late writings paradoxically involves unediting them, constellating these works not as still points of meaning or as incorruptible texts but, rather, as *events* and phenomena of freedom.

CHAPTER 3

Dickinson's Poetic Themes

Dickinson's Poems Lack Essential Elements

R.P. Blackmur

R.P. Blackmur is considered one of the twentieth century's leading literary critics. In this excerpt from his 1937 essay "Emily Dickinson: Notes on Prejudice and Fact," Blackmur explains why he considers some of Dickinson's poems good but few, if any, great.

Like T.S. Eliot, Ezra Pound, and others associated with New Criticism (a still-influential literary movement that attempts to isolate individual works of literature from a writer's personal, cultural, or historical influences), Blackmur evaluates Dickinson's poems largely on the basis of the poet's adherence to certain formal conventions. Examples of such conventions are consistent use of imagery and metaphor, a logical progression of ideas toward one main theme, and precision of language, including word order.

Though Blackmur finds Dickinson's poems lacking in the essential classic elements, he does find them rich in insight, honesty, and originality, a series of happy "accidents" that helps explain the poet's appeal.

Over two-thirds of Emily Dickinson's nine hundred odd printed poems are exercises, and no more, some in the direction of poetry, and some not. The object is usually in view, though some of the poems are but exercises in pursuit of an unknown object, but the means of attainment are variously absent, used in error, or ill-chosen. The only weapon constantly in use is ... the natural aptitude for language; and it is hardly surprising to find that that weapon, used alone and against great odds, should occasionally produce an air of frantic strain instead of strength, of conspicuous

From R.P. Blackmur, "Emily Dickinson: Notes on Prejudice and Fact," in *Language as Gesture* by R.P. Blackmur (New York: Harcourt Brace Jovanovich, 1952). Reprinted by permission of the Estate of R.P. Blackmur.

oddity instead of indubitable rightness.

Let us take for a first example a reasonably serious poem on one of the dominant Dickinson themes, the obituary theme of the great dead—a theme to which [American novelists Nathaniel] Hawthorne and Henry James were equally addicted—and determine if we can where its failure lies.

> More life went out, when He went
> Than ordinary breath,
> Lit with a finer phosphor
> Requiring in the quench
>
> A power of renownéd cold—
> The climate of the grave
> A temperature just adequate
> So anthracite to live.
>
> For some an ampler zero,
> A frost more needle keen
> Is necessary to reduce
> The Ethiop within.
>
> Others extinguish easier—
> A gnat's minutest fan
> Sufficient to obliterate
> A tract of citizen.

The first thing to notice—a thing characteristic of exercises—is that the order or plot of the elements of the poem is not that of a complete poem; the movement of the parts is downward and toward a disintegration of the effect wanted. A good poem so constitutes its parts as at once to contain them and to deliver or release by the psychological force of their sequence the full effect only when the poem is done. Here the last quatrain is obviously wrongly placed; it comes like an afterthought, put in to explain why the third stanza was good. It should have preceded the third stanza, and perhaps with the third stanza—both of course in revised form—might have come at the very beginning, or perhaps in suspension between the first and second stanzas. Such suggestions throw the poem into disorder; actually the disorder is already there. It is not the mere arrangement of stanzas that is at fault; the units in disorder are deeper in the material, perhaps in the compositional elements of the conception, perhaps in the executive elements of the image-words used to afford circulation to the poem, perhaps elsewhere in the devices not used but wanted. The point for emphasis is that it is hard to believe that a conscientious poet could have failed to see that no amount of correction and polish could raise this exercise to the condition of a mature poem. The material is all there—the inspiration and the language; what it requires is a thorough revision—a re-seeing calculated to compose in objective form the immediacy and singleness of effect which the poet no doubt herself felt.

Perhaps we may say—though the poem is not near so bad an example as many—that the uncomposed disorder is accepted by the poet because the poem was itself written automatically. To the sensitive hand and expectant ear words will arrange themselves, however gotten hold of, and seem to breed by mere contact. The brood is the meaning we catch up to. Is not this really automatic writing *tout court?* Most of the Dickinson poems seem to have been initially as near automatic writing as may be. The bulk remained automatic, subject to correction and multiplication of detail. Others, which reach intrinsic being, have been patterned, inscaped, injected one way or another with the elan or elixir of the poet's dominant attitudes. The poem presently examined remains too much in the automatic choir; the elan is there, which is why we examine it at all, but without the additional advantage of craft it fails to carry everything before it.

WORD CHOICES UNINTELLIGIBLE

The second stanza of the poem is either an example of automatic writing unrelieved, or is an example of bad editing, or both. Its only meaning is in the frantic strain toward meaning—a strain so frantic that all responsibility toward the shapes and primary significance of words was ignored. "A temperature just adequate / So Anthracite to live" even if it were intelligible, which it is not, would be beyond bearing awkward to read. It is not bad grammar alone that works ill; words sometimes make their own grammar good on the principle of ineluctable association—when the association forces the words into meaning. Here we have [an arbitrary word choice]. The word *anthracite* is the crux of the trouble. Anthracite is coal; is hard, is black, gives heat, and has a rushing crisp sound; it has a connection with carbuncle and with a fly-borne disease of which one symptom resembles a carbuncle; it is stratified in the earth, is formed of organic matter as a consequence of enormous pressure through geologic time; etc., etc. One or several of these senses may contribute to the poem; but because the context does not denominate it, it does not appear which. My own guess is that Emily Dickinson wanted the effect of something hard and cold and perhaps black and took *anthracite* off the edge of her vocabulary largely because she liked the sound. This is another way of saying that *anthracite* is an irresponsible product of her aptitude for language. . . .

Another nice question is involved in the effect of the *order* of the verbs used to represent the point of death: *quench, reduce, extinguish, obliterate.* The question is, are not these verbs pretty nearly interchangeable? Would not any other verb of destructive action do just as well? In short, is there any word in this poem which either fits or contributes to the association at all exactly? I think not—with the single exception of "phosphor."

The burden of these observations on words will I hope have made itself plain; it is exactly the burden of the observations on the form of the whole poem. The poem is an exercise whichever way you take it: an approach to the organization of its material but by no means a complete organization. It is almost a rehearsal—a doing over of something not done—and a variation of stock intellectual elements in an effort to accomplish an adventure in feeling. The reader can determine for himself—if he can swallow . . . the anthracite . . .—how concrete and actual the adventure was made. . . .

Let us present two more examples and stop. We have the word *plush* in different poems as follows. "One would as soon assault a plush or violate a star . . . Time's consummate plush . . . A dog's belated feet like intermittent plush . . . We step like plush, we stand like snow . . . Sentences of plush." The word is on the verge of bursting with wrong meaning, and on account of the bursting, the stress with which the poet employed it, we are all prepared to accept it, and indeed do accept it, when suddenly we realize the wrongness, that "plush" was not what was meant at all, but was a substitute for it. The word has been distorted but not transformed on the page; which is to say it is not in substantial control. Yet it is impossible not to believe that to Emily Dickinson's ear it meant what it said and what could not otherwise be said.

The use of the word *purple* is another example of a word's getting out of control through the poet's failure to maintain an objective feeling of responsibility toward language. We have, in different poems, a "purple host" meaning "soldiers";

"purple territories," associated with salvation in terms of "Pizarro's shores"; "purple" meaning "dawn"; a "purple finger" probably meaning "shadow"; a purple raveling of cloud at sunset; ships of purple on seas of daffodil; the sun quenching in purple; a purple brook; purple traffic; a peacock's purple train, purple none can avoid—meaning death; no suitable purple to put on the hills; a purple tar wrecked in peace, the purple well of eternity; the purple or royal state of a corpse; the Purple of Ages; a sowing of purple seed which is inexplicable; the purple of the summer; the purple wheel of faith; day's petticoat of purple; etc., etc. Taken cumulatively, this is neither a distortion nor a transformation of sense; it is very near an obliteration of everything but a favorite sound, meaning something desirable, universal, distant, and immediate. I choose the word as an example not because it is particularly bad—it is not, it is relatively harmless—but because it is typical and happens to be easy to follow in unexpanded quotation. It is thoroughly representative of Emily Dickinson's habit of so employing certain favorite words that their discriminated meanings tend to melt into the single sentiment of self-expression. We can feel the sentiment but we have lost the meaning. The willing reader can see for himself the analogous process taking place—with slightly different final flavors—in word after word: for example in the words *dateless, pattern, compass, circumference, ecstasy, immortality, white, ruby, crescent, peninsula,* and *spice.* The meanings become the conventions of meanings, the asserted agreement that meaning is there. That is the end toward which Emily Dickinson worked, willy-nilly, in her words. If you can accept the assertion for the sake of the knack—not the craft—with which it is made you will be able to read much more of her work than if you insist on actual work done.

THREE SAVING ACCIDENTS

But there were, to repeat and to conclude, three saving accidents at work in the body of Emily Dickinson's work sufficient to redeem in fact a good many poems to the state of their original intention. There was the accident of cultural crisis, the skeptical faith and desperately experimental mood, which both released and drove the poet's sensibility to express the crisis personally. There was the accident that the poet had so great an aptitude for language that it could seldom be completely lost in the conventional formulas to-

ward which her meditating mind ran. And there was the
third accident that the merest self-expression, or the merest
statement of recognition or discrimination or vision, may
sometimes also be, by the rule of unanimity and a common
tongue, its best objective expression.

When two or more of the accidents occur simultaneously
a poem or a fragment of a poem may be contrived. . . .

> Presentiment is that long shadow on the lawn
> Indicative that suns go down;
> The notice to the startled grass
> That darkness is about to pass.

If the reader compares this poem with Andrew Marvell's
classic poem "To His Coy Mistress," he will see what can be
gotten out of the same theme when fully expanded. The difference is of magnitude; the magnitude depends on craft;
the Dickinson poem stops, Marvell's is completed. What
happens when the poem does not stop may be shown in the
following example of technical and moral confusion.

> I got so I could hear his name
> Without—
> Tremendous gain!
> That stop-sensation in my soul,
> And thunder in the room.
>
> I got so l could walk across
> That angle in the floor
> Where he turned—so—and I turned how—
> And all our sinew tore.
>
> I got so I could stir the box
> In which his letters grew—
> Without that forcing in my breath
> As staples driven through.
>
> Could dimly recollect a Grace—
> I think they called it "God,"
> Renowned to ease extremity
> When formula had failed—
>
> And shape my hands petition's way—
> Tho' ignorant of word
> That Ordination utters—
> My business with the cloud.
>
> If any Power behind it be
> Not subject to despair,
> To care in some remoter way
> For so minute affair
> As misery—

Itself too vast for interrupting more,
Supremer than—
Superior to—

Nothing is more remarkable than the variety of inconsis-
tency this effort displays. The first three stanzas are at one
level of sensibility and of language and are as good verse as
Emily Dickinson ever wrote. The next two stanzas are on a
different and fatigued level of sensibility, are bad verse and
flat language, and have only a serial connection with the first
three. The last stanza, if it is a stanza, is on a still different
level of sensibility and not on a recognizable level of language at all: the level of desperate inarticulateness to which
no complete response can be articulated in return. One
knows from the strength of the first three stanzas what might
have been meant to come after and one feels like writing the
poem oneself—the basest of all critical temptations. We feel
that Emily Dickinson let herself go. The accidents that provided her ability here made a contrivance which was not a
poem but a private mixture of first-rate verse, bad verse, and
something that is not verse at all. Yet—and this is the point—
this contrivance represents in epitome the whole of her
work; and whatever judgment you bring upon the epitome
you will, I think, be compelled to bring upon the whole.

No judgment is so persuasive as when it is disguised as a
statement of facts. I think it is a fact that the failure and success of Emily Dickinson's poetry were uniformly accidental
largely because of the private and eccentric nature of her relation to the business of poetry. She was neither a professional poet nor an amateur; she was a private poet who
wrote indefatigably as some women cook or knit. Her gift for
words and the cultural predicament of her time drove her to
poetry instead of antimacassars. Neither her personal education nor the habit of her society as she knew it ever gave
her the least inkling that poetry is a rational and objective
art and most so when the theme is self-expression. She
came, as critic Allen Tate says, at the right time for one kind
of poetry: the poetry of sophisticated, eccentric vision. That
is what makes her good—in a few poems and many passages representatively great. But she never undertook the
great profession of controlling the means of objective expression. That is why the bulk of her verse is not representative but mere fragmentary indicative notation. The pity of
it is that the document her whole work makes shows noth-

ing so much as that she had the themes, the insight, the observation, and the capacity for honesty, which had she only known how—or only known why—would have made the major instead of the minor fraction of her verse genuine poetry. But her dying society had no tradition by which to teach her the one lesson she did not know by instinct.

Emily Dickinson's Vision of "Circumference"

Jane Langton

Writer Jane Langton has collaborated with artist
Nancy Ekholm Burkert in an attempt to see Dickinson's poetry as part of a larger artistic circle and asserts that Dickinson's "odd" lifestyle was essential to
her message as a poet.

The word *circumference*, as Dickinson used it, represented not only a philosophy of the poet's art, but a
state of her "well-roundedness," a result of bold ex-
perimentation she conducted in the language of her
poetry and letters. This well-roundedness may seem
ironic to those who look only on the surface of Dickinson's isolated life. Though she avoided attending
lectures or meetings with others, she carefully scru-
tinized the details of her inner life and those of the
world immediately around her.

Throughout her life Emily Dickinson was conscious of
gaps—between childhood and maturity, girlhood and the
"translation" of marriage, the lover and the loved, "no hope"
and "hope," the living and the dead, time and eternity. In her
poetry there is a perpetual sense of separation, of reaching
across an impassable gulf, of crossing a shaking bridge, of
hammering at a door that is locked and sealed. One feels that
if she could only stretch her hand across the abyss, totter to
the other side of the bridge, and fling open the door, then
somehow she could unite the two separated things. If only by
the main strength of her two fists she could pull them together, then she could achieve her object, "circumference," a
rapturous state of suspended fulfillment and perfection.

She staked her Feathers—Gained an Arc—
Debated—Rose again—

From commentary by Jane Langton in *Acts of Light: Poems by Emily Dickinson*
(Boston: New York Graphic Society, 1980). Reprinted by permission of the author and
Little, Brown & Company.

This time—beyond the estimate
Of Envy, or of Men—

And now, among Circumference—
Her steady Boat be seen—
At home—among the Billows—As
The Bough where she was born—

Like a bird she has described a daring arc upon the air, and
this time she has completed the circle. She exists at last
(whether by exaltation, or by resurrection after death) in a
state of bliss called circumference. With the same reverence
she uses the word "sum" as another precious totality, in
which the random cluttered parts of life, as unlike as apples
and oranges, as impossible as an incorruptible soul in a cor-
ruptible body, could be added together into a single whole.

But how? How to close the circle, find the sum? In spite of
abysses, Alps, doors with "hasps of steel," there was a kind
of circumference that was always available to her, one sum
that could be achieved at will: the closed circle of a finished
poem, the sum of a few perfect stanzas. In the practice of her
art there was a kind of seamless perfection like that of the
eternal note of the bird's song. . . .

TOWARD A ROUNDED PERFECTION

It was as an artist seeking this kind of rounded perfection
that Emily Dickinson withdrew from society. Her solitude
was imperative, but to her contemporaries it looked curious
and queerly unconventional.

Thomas Wentworth Higginson first encountered it in
1869, when he sent her a bland invitation to hear him speak
at the Boston Woman's Club on the Greek goddesses. "You
must come down to Boston sometimes? All ladies do."

Emily must have smiled. She issued a counter-invitation,
"Could it please your convenience to come so far as Amherst
I should be very glad," and wrapped her remoteness about
her: "I do not cross my Father's ground to any House or town."

Emily Dickinson was not like "all ladies." Lectures on the
goddesses did not interest her. There was too much to do at
home, too much of first importance, too much that could not
be delayed. Her priorities were like those of Thoreau, who
thought it not worth his while to go around the world "to
count the cats in Zanzibar," who urged his readers to explore "the private sea, the Atlantic and Pacific Ocean of one's
being alone." Emily Dickinson had no need to go to Boston.

There were her own interior spaces to examine:

> Soto! Explore thyself!
> Therein thyself shalt find
> The "Undiscovered Continent"
> No Settler had the Mind.

Her chamber was not a refuge of timid hiding, but a pioneering frontier, a place of adventure. Often the floor of that upstairs room became a watery deep on which she was swept out to sea—

Among the children to whom Emily Dickinson was a presence rather than an absence was [her niece] Matty, who was treated to this vivid explanation of her Aunt Emily's runaway escapes to the privacy of her own room: "She would stand looking down, one hand raised, thumb and forefinger closed on an imaginary key, and say, with a quick turn of her wrist, 'It's just a turn—and freedom, Matty!'"

Her Own Standard of Measure

In her lifetime Emily Dickinson's poems were generally thought too odd for public print. Odd they remain, but with the singularity of genius. Her distortions of the language are an example of her uniqueness. Her English is her own invention, a curious dialect in which parts of speech are wrenched and forced into outlandish shapes to fit a higher grammar that is hers alone. Adjectives are driven to dizzy extremes: "Admirabler Show," "The Birds jocoser sung." Almost any word can become an exotic negative: "Swerveless Tune," "Perturbless Plan." Words that don't fit are simply omitted:

> How dare I therefore, stint a faith
> On which so [much that is] vast depends—

And where common usage might call for the declarative mood, Emily Dickinson's poems often riot in a rampaging, giddy, transubstantiated subjunctive:

> Without the Snow's Tableau
> Winter, were lie—to me—
> Because I see—New Englandly—

We can see the method in her skewed syntax in a poem about the sound of the wind:

> Inheritance, it is, to us—
> Beyond the Art to Earn—
> Beyond the trait to take away
> By Robber, since the Gain
> Is gotten not of fingers—
> And inner than the Bone—

The simple adjective "inner" has been pushed into a corner where, by the lucky accident that it happens to end in "er," it seems to mean "more inner," like a comparative. Thus her use of "than" has a bizarre correctness. The phrase succeeds and the reader feels a twinge in the marrow.

A LETTER TO DR. AND MRS. J.G. HOLLAND

Dickinson's perception of life and its events as evolving in a circular manner is illustrated in this excerpt from a letter the poet sent to Dr. and Mrs. J.G. Holland in 1853. As Dickinson describes herself returning, circlelike, to the same events over and over again, the world itself begins to appear fuller and more circular to Dickinson as well. The complete letter can be found in Mabel Loomis Todd's collection Letters of Emily Dickinson.

If it wasn't for broad daylight, and cooking-stoves, and roosters, I'm afraid you would have occasion to smile at my letters often, but so sure as "this mortal" essays immortality, a crow from a neighboring farm-yard dissipates the illusion, and I am here again.

And what I mean is this—that I thought of you all last week, until the world grew rounder than it sometimes is, and I broke several dishes.

Monday, I solemnly resolved I would be *sensible*, so I wore thick shoes, and thought of Dr. Humphrey, and the Moral Law. One glimpse of *The Republican* makes me break things again—I read in it every night.

Her meter too is distinctive. At first glance it looks simple. Over and over again, three and four beats alternate in four-line quatrains:

This is my letter to the World
That never wrote to Me—
The simple News that Nature told—
With tender Majesty

In many poems two lines of three beats are followed by a line of four beats and a final line of three:

I stepped from Plank to Plank
A slow and cautious way
The Stars about my Head I felt
About my Feet the Sea.

These homely rhythms have been traced to the meters of the hymns Emily Dickinson must have sung in church, hymns like this one by Isaac Watts:

> Come, sound his Praise abroad,
> And hymns of Glory sing:
> Jehovah is the Sovereign God,
> The universal King.

She may also have studied hymn meters more carefully in her father's copy of Watts's *Christian Psalmody*. But Emily Dickinson was too original to be content for long with anyone else's rules. Sometimes she took daring liberties with the pat rhythms of the hymns, breaking the singsong meters to suit her meaning:

> Just lost, when I was saved!
> Just felt the world go by!
> Just girt me for the onset with Eternity,
> When breath blew back,
> And on the other side
> I heard recede the disappointed tide!

To Thomas Wentworth Higginson this sort of dramatic irregularity was "uncontrolled," and he reproved her "spasmodic" gait. Nor was he the only one to be put off by her lopsided rhythms and bold ways with rhyme, by lines that matched "pearl" with "bowl," "blood" with "dead," "plucking" with "morning." In her lifetime only a handful of poems by Emily Dickinson was published (all anonymously), although the newspapers and popular journals of her day regularly printed hosts of sentimental verses by less talented women. Perhaps it was because Lizzie Lincoln and Fanny Fern and Grace Greenwood and Minnie Myrtle could be trusted to make pretty twins of all their rhymes and jingle their meters more dependably. Even so august a poet as Oliver Wendell Holmes was grateful to the friend who altered his rhyming at the last minute before going to press, changing his careless matching of "gone" with "forlorn" to a tidier "gone" and "wan."

Reading the doggerel that appeared day after day, year in and year out, in the newspaper edited by Samuel Bowles, Emily must have wondered at it. Jokingly she complained to Higginson of being "the only Kangaroo among the Beauty, Sir."

She was not to be a beauty to Higginson until after her death. His lack of perception has been explained by Dickinson scholar Thomas Johnson: "He was trying to measure a cube by the rules of plane geometry."

Dickinson Acquired a Unique Understanding of Faith

Richard Wilbur

When Emily Dickinson, at age seventeen, refused to stand at a Mount Holyoke revival meeting and declare herself a Christian, she was the only one among her classmates to so refuse. Yet her poems and letters have always revealed a deeply religious nature. Distinguished poet Richard Wilbur, winner of both the Pulitzer Prize and the National Book Award, uncovers a logic to the unorthodox beliefs of a writer who wrote much about both faith and hypocrisy.

The poems of Emily Dickinson are a continual appeal to experience, motivated by an arrogant passion for the truth. "Truth is so rare a thing," she once said, "it is delightful to tell." And, sending some poems to Colonel Higginson, she wrote, "Excuse them, if they are untrue." And again, to the same correspondent, she observed, "Candor is the only wile"—meaning that the writer's bag of tricks need contain one trick only, the trick of being honest. That her taste for truth involved a regard for objective fact need not be argued: we have her poem on the snake, and that on the humming-bird, and they are small masterpieces of exact description. She liked accuracy; she liked solid and homely detail; and even in her most exalted poems we are surprised and reassured by buckets, shawls, or buzzing flies.

But her chief truthfulness lay in her insistence on discovering the facts of her inner experience. She was a Linnaeus to the phenomena of her own consciousness, describing and distinguishing the states and motions of her soul. The results of this "psychic reconnaissance," as [critic George F.] Whicher called it, were several. For one thing, it made her articulate about inward matters which poetry had never so

Excerpted from "Sumptuous Destitution" by Richard Wilbur, in *Emily Dickinson: Three Views* (Amherst, MA: Amherst College Press, 1960). Reprinted by permission of Amherst College Press.

sharply defined; specifically, it made her capable of writing two such lines as these:

A perfect, paralyzing bliss
Contented as despair.

We often assent to the shock of a paradox before we understand it, but those lines are so just and so concentrated as to explode their meaning instantly in the mind. They did not come so easily, I think, to Emily Dickinson. Unless I guess wrongly as to chronology, such lines were the fruit of long poetic research; the poet had worked toward them through much study of the way certain emotions can usurp consciousness entirely, annulling our sense of past and future, cancelling near and far, converting all time and space to a joyous or grievous here and now. It is in their ways of annihilating time and space that bliss and despair are comparable.

Which leads me to a second consequence of Emily Dickinson's self-analysis. It is one thing to assert as pious doctrine that the soul has power, with God's grace, to master circumstance. It is another thing to find out personally, as Emily Dickinson did in writing her psychological poems, that the aspect of the world is in no way constant, that the power of external things depends on our state of mind, that the soul selects its own society and may, if granted strength to do so, select a superior order and scope of consciousness which will render it finally invulnerable. She learned these things by witnessing her own courageous spirit.

THREE MAIN PRIVATIONS

Another result of Emily Dickinson's introspection was that she discovered some grounds, in the nature of her soul and its affections, for a personal conception of such ideas as Heaven and Immortality, and so managed a precarious convergence between her inner experience and her religious inheritance. What I want to attempt now is a rough sketch of the imaginative logic by which she did this. I had better say before I start that I shall often seem demonstrably wrong, because Emily Dickinson, like many poets, was consistent in her concerns but inconsistent in her attitudes. The following, therefore, is merely an opinion as to her main drift.

Emily Dickinson never lets us forget for very long that in some respects life gave her short measure; and indeed it is possible to see the greater part of her poetry as an effort to cope with her sense of privation. I think that for her there

were three major privations: she was deprived of an orthodox and steady religious faith; she was deprived of love; she
was deprived of literary recognition.

At the age of 17, after a series of revival meetings at Mount
Holyoke Seminary, Emily Dickinson found that she must
refuse to become a professing Christian. To some modern
minds this may seem to have been a sensible and necessary
step; and surely it was a step toward becoming such a poet
as she became. But for her, no pleasure in her own integrity
could then eradicate the feeling that she had betrayed a de-
ficiency, a want of grace. In her letters to Abiah Root she
tells of the enhancing effect of conversion on her fellow-
students, and says of herself in a famous passage:

> *I* am one of the lingering bad ones, and so do I slink away,
> and pause and ponder, and ponder and pause, and do work
> without knowing why, not surely, for this brief world, and
> more sure it is not for heaven, and I ask what this message
> *means* that they ask for so very eagerly: *you* know of this
> depth and fulness, will you try to tell me about it?

There is humor in that, and stubbornness, and a bit of
characteristic lurking pride: but there is also an anguished
sense of having separated herself, through some dry inca-
pacity, from spiritual community, from purpose, and from
magnitude of life. As a child of evangelical Amherst, she inevitably thought of purposive, heroic life as requiring a vigorous faith. Out of such a thought she later wrote:

> The abdication of Belief
> Makes the Behavior small—
> Better an ignis fatuus
> Than no illume at all—

That hers was a species of religious personality goes
without saying; but by her refusal of such ideas as original
sin, redemption, hell, and election, she made it impossible
for herself—as Whicher observed—"to share the religious
life of her generation." She became an unsteady congregation of one.

Her second privation, the privation of love, is one with
which her poems and her biographies have made us ex-
ceedingly familiar, though some biographical facts remain
conjectural. She had the good fortune, at least once, to be-
stow her heart on another; but she seems to have found her
life, in great part, a history of loneliness, separation, and
bereavement.

As for literary fame, some will deny that Emily Dickinson ever greatly desired it, and certainly there is evidence mostly from her latter years, to support such a view. She *did* write that "Publication is the auction/ Of the mind of man." And she *did* say to Helen Hunt Jackson, "How can you print a piece of your soul?" But earlier, in 1861, she had frankly expressed to Sue Dickinson the hope that "sometime" she might make her kinfolk proud of her. The truth is, I think, that Emily Dickinson knew she was good, and began her career with a normal appetite for recognition. I think that she later came, with some reason, to despair of being understood or properly valued, and so directed against her hopes of fame what was by then a well-developed disposition to renounce. That she wrote a good number of poems about fame supports my view: the subjects to which a poet returns are those which vex him.

Distant Desires Create Intense Longings

What did Emily Dickinson do, as a poet, with her sense of privation? . . .

[She] elected the economy of desire, and called her privation good, rendering it positive by renunciation. And so she came to live in a huge world of delectable distances. Far-off words like "Brazil" or "Circassian" appear continually in her poems as symbols or things distanced by loss or renunciation, yet infinitely prized and yearned-for. So identified in her mind are distance and delight that, when ravished by the sight of a hummingbird in her garden, she calls it "the mail from Tunis." And not only are the objects of her desire distant; they are also very often moving away, their sweetness increasing in proportion to their remoteness. "To disappear enhances," one of the poems begins, and another closes with these lines:

> The Mountain—at a given distance—
> In Amber—lies—
> Approached—the Amber flits—a little—
> And That's—the Skies—

To the eye of desire, all things are seen in a profound perspective, either moving or gesturing toward the vanishing-point. Or to use a figure which may be closer to Miss Dickinson's thought, to the eye of desire the world is a centrifuge, in which all things are straining or flying toward the occult circumference. In some such way, Emily Dickinson conceived her world, and it was in a spatial metaphor that she gave her personal definition of Heaven. "Heaven," she said, "is what I cannot reach."

At times it seems that there is nothing in her world but her own soul, with its attendant abstraction, and, at a vast remove, the inscrutable Heaven. On most of what might intervene she has closed the valves of her attention, and what mortal objects she does acknowledge are riddled by desire to the point of transparency. Here is a sentence from her correspondence: "Enough is of so vast a sweetness, I suppose it never occurs, only pathetic counterfeits." The writer of that sentence could not invest her longings in any finite object. Again she wrote, "Emblem is immeasurable—that is why it is better than fulfillment, which can be drained." For such a sensibility, it was natural and necessary that things be touched with infinity. Therefore her nature poetry, when most serious, does not play descriptively with birds or flowers but presents us repeatedly with dawn, noon, and sunset, those grand ceremonial moments of the day which argue the splendor of Paradise. Or it shows us the ordinary landscape transformed by the electric brilliance of a storm; or it shows us the fields succumbing to the annual mystery of death. In her love-poems, Emily Dickinson was at first covetous of the [unnamed] beloved himself; indeed, she could be idolatrous, going so far as to say that his face, should she see it again in Heaven, would eclipse the face of Jesus. But in what I take to be her later work the beloved's lineaments, which were never very distinct, vanish entirely; he becomes pure emblem, a symbol of remote spiritual joy, and so is all but absorbed into the idea of Heaven. The lost beloved is, as one poem declares, "infinite when gone," and in such lines as the following we are aware of him mainly as an instrument in the poet's commerce with the beyond.

Of all the Souls that stand create—
I have elected—One—
When Sense from Spirit—flies away—
And Subterfuge—is done—
When that which is—and that which was—
Apart—intrinsic—stand—
And this brief Tragedy of Flesh—
Is shifted—like a Sand—
When Figures show their royal Front—
And Mists—are carved away,
Behold the Atom—I preferred—
To all the lists of Clay!

RENUNCIATION LEADS TO DIVINE HAPPINESS

. . . One psychic experience which she interpreted as beatitude was "glee," or as some would call it, euphoria. Now a notable thing about glee or euphoria is its gratuitousness. It seems to come from nowhere, and it was this apparent sourcelessness of the emotion from which Emily Dickinson made her inference. "The 'happiness' without a cause," she said, "is the best happiness, for glee intuitive and lasting is the gift of God." Having foregone all earthly causes of happiness, she could only explain her glee, when it came, as a divine gift—a compensation in joy for what she had renounced in satisfaction, and a foretaste of the mood of Heaven. The experience of glee, as she records it, is boundless: all distances collapse, and the soul expands to the very circumference of things. Here is how she put it in one of her letters: "Abroad is close tonight and I have but to lift my hands to touch the 'Hights of Abraham.'" And one of her gleeful poems begins,

'Tis little—I could care for Pearls—
Who own the ample sea—

How often she felt that way we cannot know, and it hardly matters. As Robert Frost has pointed out, happiness can make up in height for what it lacks in length; and the important thing for us, as for her, is that she construed the experience as a divine gift. So also she thought of the power to write poetry, a power which, as we know, came to her often; and poetry must have been the chief source of her sense of blessedness. The poetic impulses which visited her seemed "bulletins from Immortality," and by their means she converted all her losses into gains, and all the pains of her life to that clarity and repose which were to her the qualities of Heaven.

Emily Dickinson's Feminist Humor

Suzanne Juhasz, Christanne Miller,
and Martha Nell Smith

Her humor often underestimated by critics and biographers, Emily Dickinson is usually portrayed as a tragic figure haunted by personal demons. But though her poems deal with serious personal issues, they show a public awareness that is often displayed with humor.

In her animal poems, for example, nonhuman characters amplify various social roles, a technique that not only precedes that of American poet Ogden Nash by nearly a hundred years but shows that she is deeply aware of her own limited social role, as well.

In their book *The Comic Power in Emily Dickinson*, from which this excerpt is taken, Suzanne Juhasz, Christanne Miller, and Martha Nell Smith argue that Dickinson's political humor is best appreciated in light of her perspective as a white, middleclass woman keenly aware of the expectations placed on a woman writer in her era.

Although Emily Dickinson was a noted wit in her circle of friends and family, and although her poetry is surely clever, frequently downright funny, and, as we shall argue, throughout possessed of a significant comic vision, criticism has paid little attention to her humor. Dickinson's profound scrutiny of life-and-death matters has usually taken precedence in the analysis and evaluation of her work. Yet comedy is a part of that profundity, and this volume brings the comic aspects of her vision to center stage for the first time. It is no coincidence that feminist critics have chosen this subject, for comedy is aligned with subversive and disruptive modes that offer alternative perspectives on culture. But even as it is a cliché in American social politics that "feminists have no sense of humor," so the comedy specifically associated with women's critique of patriarchy is often overlooked.

A feminist critical approach to Dickinson's comedy reveals a poet whose topic and audience are larger than herself. It shows how Dickinson critiques the established culture through language forms that stress their status as performance and demand the participation of an audience. In particular, focusing on comedy highlights her responses as a nineteenth-century upper-middle-class woman to situations in which she is both attracted to and angered by patriarchal power, situations in which she critiques contemporary institutions, and situations in which she feels suffocated by social conventions. Through formal elements of voice, image, and narrative, Dickinson teases, mocks, even outrages her audience in ways that are akin both to the gestures of traditional comedy and to specifically feminist humor. In short, Dickinson's comedy is not contained by poems that are obviously funny but pervades her writing to offer a transforming vision of the world.

Dickinson the tragedienne, however, has by now received so much press that this role has become a norm in critical representations of her, in feminist as well as traditional readings. George Whicher, setting the tone for contemporary receptions of Dickinson, writes in 1938, "by mastery of her suffering she won a sanity that could make even grief a plaything." Thus, this critical story goes, Dickinson is a heroine *because* she suffered so, and because she gave us great poetry out of this suffering. Not all subsequent critics have been so charitable about the triumph of her fragile sanity, but most agree that her despair and desolation are the crucible in which her poetry is forged. Whicher proposes a compensatory, even therapeutic theory for Dickinson's poetry:

> In projecting her intensest feelings on paper she was finding a form of relief in action; she was, in Emerson's phrase, "grinding into paint" her burden of despair. So she was enabled to fulfill the prescript of her generation for utter rectitude of conduct, which for her meant the stifling of hopes, and yet keep the bitter waters from stagnating in her breast. Though her mental balance was unsteady for some years to come, she achieved and held it.

Such an approach makes the relation of art to biography a closed circuit. There is no audience; or, more properly, the poet's audience is herself. Life experiences govern the experience that is the poem, mediated only in that the poem is seen not simply to describe but to offer a degree of control over them. Without reference, then, to the performance aspect of the literary act, that is, to the complex function of any poem, such critics end by simplifying not only the affective purpose of the poem but its content as well.

ONE READER'S COMIC RESPONSE

This anonymous limerick was found in an old publication and reprinted in Dickinson Studies #78: Emily Dickinson in Public.

> There once was a poet named Emily
> who lived in the heart of her family.
> She never went out
> but lived without doubt
> on metaphor, symbol and simile.

As we might expect, critics who focus on the direct link between biography and poetry are especially prone to emphasize the tragedic elements of Dickinson's art. To take three important examples in more recent criticism, John Cody, Paula Bennett, and Vivian Pollak—for all of their ideological differences and notwithstanding the forty-years' span their works cover—have reinforced a sense of Dickinson as tragic heroine. . . .

ROLE OF THE AUDIENCE DIMINISHED

We do not argue here that there are no tragic elements in Dickinson's life or art. We take issue, however, with the totality or one-dimensionality of the position. It edits out the wry, the witty, the playful, the tough, the challenging, the successful Dickinson. Moreover, it takes Dickinson all too literally, ignoring her own directives about reading and writing: "Tell all the Truth but tell it slant—/ Success in Circuit lies." Telling it slant implies the participation in the poetic act of voice, gesture, posture, attitude, and style. It implies, in other words, the necessity of performance, so that the poem cannot be seen as *simply* the compulsive outpouring of powerful feelings. Life experience—all the Truth—has been crafted and shaped for some purpose, and a corollary to the fact that the words are performed is that some audience is anticipated. The poem's affective purpose has to do with a reader as well as with the poet herself.

Comedy becomes possible in a poetics of this kind. To begin with, comedy stresses the role of the audience and its response to the joke. Additionally, comedy implies commentary: the comedienne's art is always slant, never wholly caught up in a feeling or a situation. From this perspective we can see how Dickinson critiques her subject as much as she embodies it. Comedy implies, as well, winning rather than losing, the affirmation of life rather than its destruction. These elements do exist in Dickinson's poetry, and taking her slant, or allowing for her comic perspective, enables us to experience them. . . .

The extent to which one *finds* Dickinson funny, or feminist, depends on several factors. First, because much of Dickinson's comic vision stems from her gender consciousness, it is difficult to separate that consciousness, or her feminism, from her humor. To appreciate the full range of Dickinson's humor, one must be able to conceive of her as a sharp critic of her world, as a self-conscious writer identifying with (at least white middle-class) women's experience as a basis for social criticism, and as a crafter of multiple levels of intention in her poems. In contrast, to the extent that one envisions this poet as unconscious of her self and her craft, or as a victim suffering under tyrannical parents, patriarchy generally, or her own neuroses, one will not find humor in her poems. . . .

POEMS SHOW AWARENESS IN EXAGGERATION

In "I'm Nobody! Who are you?" for example, the speaker coyly introduces herself as charmingly unimportant. Here the poet mocks the pretensions of the public world by imagining public figures as loud bullfrogs and herself as someone unrecognizable to the crowd

> I'm Nobody! Who are you?
> Are you—Nobody—Too?
> Then there's a pair of us!
> Don't tell! they'd advertise—you know!
>
> How dreary—to be—Somebody!
> How public—like a Frog—
> To tell one's name—the livelong June—
> To an admiring Bog!

The audience who would appreciate one's announcement of

self-importance has the character of a swamp, something one sinks in, not something with an opinion to be respected. Similarly, being "Somebody" in the terms of this poem constitutes self-advertisement (telling one's own name) or allowing others to "advertise" for you—that is, identity in this context is a result of staged marketing rather than of production or worth. Any person of reasonable modesty, the poet implies, would rather be hiding out with her, another "Nobody," free from the "Bog." The apparent lack of guile in the speaker's opening playfully conspiratorial tone slides into pointed—but still apparently playful—social observation, as she rhymes "Frog" with "Bog" to describe the "Somebod[ies]" and the audience she scorns. Cuteness allows the speaker to satirize her subject sharply yet keep her charm.

"She sights a Bird—she chuckles—" contains similarly accessible comedy with the light ironic twist familiar in Dickinson's simplest comic poems.

> She sights a Bird—she chuckles—
> She flattens—then she crawls—
> She runs without the look of feet—
> Her eyes increase to Balls—
>
> Her Jaws stir—twitching—hungry—
> Her Teeth can hardly stand—
> She leaps, but Robin leaped the first—
> Ah, Pussy, of the Sand,
>
> The Hopes so juicy ripening—
> You almost bathed your Tongue—
> When Bliss disclosed a hundred Toes—
> And fled with every one—

In the first two stanzas, this marvelous portrait of the pouncing cat has the structure of comic suspense. The cat's motions, while described realistically enough to be immediately recognizable, exaggerate each of her movements so that the "Pussy" is cartoon-like, a figure that epitomizes hungry cat-ness. Then, with "Ah, Pussy, of the Sand," the narrative turns to provide a second and more speculative type of humor. The poet here redescribes the event in more abstract and metaphorical terms, thereby making it a kind of parable of the failed attempt to gain a prize. Rather than moralizing, however, Dickinson maintains the comic tone through her continued exaggeration, and by animating Hopes and Bliss. Just as you "almost bathe" your panting, salivating "Tongue"—the ultimate sign of animal desire—

"Bliss" reveals its extraordinary mobility: it "disclose[s] a hundred Toes," "every one" carrying it safely away. Here is a comic primal scene for all failure to procure "Bliss."

As both poems above indicate, animals play major roles in Dickinson's funny poems, which often function as fables that comment on human foibles by means of the poems' furred or winged subjects. The clever jingly rhymes of many of these ditties proclaim them true forerunners of Ogden Nash.

> The butterfly obtains
> But little sympathy
> Though favorably mentioned
> In Etymology—
>
> Because he travels freely
> And wears a proper coat
> The circumspect are certain
> That he is dissolute—
>
> Had he the homely scutcheon
> Of modest Industry
> 'Twere fitter certifying
> For Immortality—

This poem opposes the New England Protestant work ethic with the sly notion that nature has more liberal values for its denizens. The butterfly, a kind of playboy of the Western skies, not only has fun but looks good—both qualities destined to make him the subject of much headshaking from the good citizens of the kind of town that Dickinson knew all too well. However, in this poem, the butterfly emerges triumphant—a candidate for Immortality by means of Etymology if not Industry. The play with all those multisyllabic rhyme words—*sympathy* with *Etymology*, *coat* with *dissolute*, and *Industry* with *Immortality*—points both to the highminded seriousness of the town's morality and also to a means by which others outside of the system might mock it.

Dickinson writes about despised as well as admired creatures:

> A Rat surrendered here
> A brief career of Cheer
> And Fraud and Fear.
>
> Of Ignominy's due
> Let all addicted to
> Beware.
>
> The most obliging Trap
> It's tendency to snap
> Cannot resist—

> Temptation is the Friend
> Repugnantly resigned
> At last.

If the butterfly poem questions a too-simplistic morality, this one takes an alternative stance, interrogating an equally prevalent tendency to admire the charming rogue. Not, however, because crime doesn't pay, but because, more profoundly, the excessive egotism it engenders is in the end self-defeating. The Rat, although quite properly caught, is a comic character throughout his drama because of his anarchic bravado. The jaunty meter and playful rhymes characterize him as a cocky blend of Cheer and Fraud and Fear. His problem, however, is in thinking himself bigger than his (nonexistent) britches. There is more to the world than oneself. Rats may swagger, but traps will snap. So be it.

Naming as a Strategy in Dickinson's Poems

Sharon Cameron

Dickinson defines internal emotions as well as she describes external events. Through use of metaphor and imagistic language, the poet gives name to a specific feeling—a particular pain, for instance—as the word is experienced not in a variety of circumstances and with varying levels of intensity, but as a feeling that is specific, recognizable: "Pain—has an Element of Blank—".

Often complex, Dickinson's methods of definition present some problems for author Sharon Cameron. Because Dickinson's poems often begin with the definition rather than end with it, Cameron argues that the naming lacks the finality of the last word and leaves the reader to question its exactness. This excerpt is from Cameron's influential study *Lyric Time: Dickinson and the Limits of Genre.*

For Emily Dickinson, perhaps no more so than for the rest of us, there was a powerful discrepancy between what was "inner than the Bone—" and what could be acknowledged. To the extent that her poems are a response to that discrepancy—are, on the one hand, a defiant attempt to deny that the discrepancy poses a problem and, on the other, an admission of defeat at the problem's enormity—they have much to teach us about the way in which language articulates our life. There is indeed a sense in which these poems test the limits of what we might reveal if we tried, and also of what, despite our exertions, will not give itself over to utterance. The question of the visibility of interior experience is one that will concern me in this chapter, for it lies at the heart of what Dickinson makes present to us. In "The Dream of Communication," Geoffrey Hartman writes, "Art 'represents' a self which is either insufficiently 'present' or feels itself as not 'presentable.'" On both counts one thinks of Dickinson, for her poems disassemble the body in order to penetrate to the places where feelings lie, as if hidden, and they tell us that bodies are not barriers the way we sometimes think they are. Despite the staggering sophistication with which we discuss complex issues, like Dickinson, we have few words, if any, for what happens inside us. Perhaps this is because we have been taught to conceive of ourselves as perfectly inexplicable or, if explicable, then requiring the aid of someone else to scrutinize what we are explicating, to validate it. We have been taught that we cannot see for ourselves—this despite the current emphasis on [self-analysis]. But Dickinson tells us that we can see. More important, she tells us how to name what we see. . . .

NAMING PAIN

The most excruciating interior experience, and perhaps the most inherently nameless, is that of pain. If we leave aside for a moment, though it is hardly an irrelevant consideration, the fact that pain is private, not sharable, we see that Dickinson also insists its torture is a consequence of the ways in which it distorts perception. Again and again, she tells us that pain is atemporal and hence dislocating. It jars one's ordinary sense of oneself and the relation of that self to the world:

> Pain—expands the Time—
> Ages coil within
> The minute Circumference
> Of a single Brain—
> . . . .

And it is dogged:

> It struck me—every Day—
> The Lightning was as new
> As if the Cloud that instant slit
> And let the Fire through—
>
> It burned Me—in the Night—
> It Blistered to My Dream—
> It sickened fresh upon my sight—
> With every Morn that came—
>
> I thought that Storm—was brief—
> The Maddest—quickest by—
> But Nature lost the Date of This—
> And left it in the Sky—

In consequence, the self suffers separation from its own experience:

. . . .
And Something's odd—within—
The person that I was—
And this One—do not feel the same—
Could it be Madness—this?

The experience of the self perceived as other is a central occurrence in Dickinson's poetry, a kind of ritual enactment her speakers survive to tell about. She had called madness "The yawning Consciousness" and spoke of "a Cleaving in my Mind—/As if my Brain had split—". . .

What she needed to survive such experiences was "Pyramidal Nerve," for she knew: "Power is only Pain—/Stranded, thro' Discipline." This discipline had naming at its heart, for names specify relationships that have been lost, forgotten, or hitherto unperceived. Dickinson knew, moreover, that the power of names was in part a consequence of their ability to effect a reconciliation between a self and that aspect of it which had been rendered alien. Names were a way of remembering and accepting ownership of something that, by forgetting or refusing to know, one had previously repudiated. Metaphor, then, is a response to pain in that it closes the gap between feeling and one's identification of it. Metaphoric names are restorative in nature in that they bring one back to one's senses by acknowledging that what has been perceived by them can be familiarized through language.

But names are social as well as personal strategies. As Kenneth Burke suggests, a work of art "singles out a pattern of experience that is sufficiently representative of our social structure, that recurs sufficiently . . . for people to 'need a word for it' and to adopt an attitude toward it. Each work of art is the addition of a word to an informal dictionary." While in some respects metaphor and analogy are a last resort, they are also often all we have. In lieu of direct names we improvise or we do without. Such improvisation of course has rules, since language is in the public domain and what we have to work with is a vocabulary that is, more than one might suspect, "given." Thus, finding new names for interior experience is an ambivalent process, for on the one hand by the very insistence upon its necessity, the invention of a new name defies the social matrix. On the other hand, since articulation is a matter of social coherence, it must make reference to that matrix. Hence, naming is in need of precisely that thing which it deems inadequate.

SOME PROBLEMS WITH DICKINSON'S POETRY OF DEFINITION

Up to this point I have spoken about naming as an act that performs a function both social and personal, and I have gone so far as to make hyperbolic claims for its efficacy. But there are problems with naming in Dickinson's poetry. The names Dickinson gives us for experiences are frequently the most striking aspect of her poetry, and they occur often, as one might expect, in poems of definition. The problem they ask us to consider is precisely their relationship to the context in which they occur. Definitions in Dickinson's poems take two forms. The first group of statements contain the copula as the main verb, and their linguistic structure is some variation of the nominative plus the verb "to be" plus the rest of the predicate. The characteristics of the predicate are transferred to the nominative, and this transference becomes a fundamental aspect of the figurative language, as the following examples indicate:

> God is a distant—stately Lover—
> Mirth is the Mail of Anguish—
> Crisis is a Hair/Toward which forces creep
> The Lightning is a yellow Fork/From Tables in the sky
> Safe Despair it is that raves—/Agony is frugal.
> Water, is taught by thirst.
> Utmost is relative—/Have not or Have/Adjacent sums
> Faith—is the Pierless Bridge
> Drama's Vitallest Expression is the Common Day

The previous assertions are global in nature, encapsulating the totality or whole of the subject under scrutiny. The following group of assertions attempt to establish a single aspect or identic property of the thing being defined:

> A South Wind—has a pathos/Of individual Voice—
> Pain—has an Element of Blank—
> Remembrance has a Rear and Front—

Or they personify characteristic actions and attributes of the subject under consideration, distinguishing and so defining them:

> The Heart asks Pleasure—first—
> Absence disembodies—so does Death
> The Admirations—and Contempts—of time—/Show justest—
>   through an Open Tomb—

Many of these assertions are frankly aphoristic:

> A Charm invests a face/Imperfectly beheld—
> Perception of an object costs/Precise the Object's loss—

for in both groups, feeling and experience are abstracted from the context that prompted them, and from temporal considerations; the words are uttered in the third person present tense and may lack definite and indefinite articles, all of these strategies contributing to the speaker's authority, as they make a claim to experiential truth that transcends the limitations of personal experience. The distinctions between the two groups may seem to exist more in formulation than in function. Nonetheless, given a range of utterance, the former assertions lie at the epigrammatic extreme and occur with more frequency in the poems (it is thus with them that I shall be most concerned); the latter assertions, which appear with increased frequency in the letters, by their very admission of partiality, come closer to confessing their evolution from a particular incident or context.

The function of a successful formulation, one that says reality is one way and not another, is that it have no qualification; that it be the last word. The problem in many of Dickinson's poems is that it is the first word. It was Emerson who called proverbs "the literature of reason, or the statements of an absolute truth without qualification," and there is a sense in which statements like "Capacity to Terminate/Is a Specific Grace" or "Not 'Revelation'—'tis that waits/But our unfurnished eyes" preclude further statement because any statement will qualify them.

Hobbes, in *The Leviathan*, makes the following observation about names and definitions:

> Seeing then that truth consists in the right ordering of names in our affirmations, a man that seeketh precise truth had need to remember what every name he useth stands for . . . or else he will find himself entangled in words, as a bird in lime-twigs. . . . And therefore in geometry (which is the only science which it hath pleased God hitherto to bestow on mankind), men begin at settling the significations of their words; which settling of significations they call *definitions*, and place them in the beginning of their reckoning. (part I, chapter IV)

Geometric constructions are not, however, metaphoric ones, and it is important to note that in poems such definitional knowledge is credited best when it occurs at the end of a speaker's reckoning. Perhaps this is because, unlike Hobbes, we believe that, at least in poems, definitions are neither arbitrary nor conventionally agreed-upon assignations. Wrested from experience, they imply a choice whose nature is only made manifest by its context.

But Dickinson's names and definitions not only posit themselves at the beginning of poems, they also shrug off the need for further context, for it is difficult to acknowledge the complexity of a situation while stressing its formulaic qualities—unless the point of the formulation is to reveal complexity. In fact, definitions are often predicated on the assumption that experience can be expressed summarily as one thing. The detachable quality of some of Dickinson's lines receives comment as early as 1892 when Mabel Loomis Todd writes:

> How does the idea of an "Emily Dickinson Yearbook" strike you?... My thought is that with isolated lines from the already published poems, many of which are perfect comets of thought, and some of those wonderful epigrams from the *Letters*, together with a mass of *unpublished* lines which I should take from poems which could never be used entire, I could make the most brilliant year-book ever issued.... If I do not do it, some one else will want to, because ED abounds so in epigrams—.

One of her first biographers, George Whicher, comments: "Her states of mind were not progressive but approximately simultaneous." R.P. Blackmur summarizes the situation less charitably when he speaks of Dickinson's poems as "mere fragmentary indicative notation," and in a statement cited only in part in the Introduction, he explains himself: "The first thing to notice—a thing characteristic of exercises—is that the order or plot of the elements of the poem is not that of a complete poem; the movement of the parts is downwards and towards a disintegration of the effect wanted. A good poem so constitutes its parts as at once to contain them and to deliver or release by the psychological force of their sequence the full effect only when the poem is done." For how a poem tells the time of the experience it narrates directly determines the crucial relationship between what we might distinguish as the mechanism of that poem's closure and its true completion, which would be perceived as a "natural" end even were the utterance to continue beyond. We have different modes of reference to the movement that leads to the coincidence of closure and internal completion within a given poem. We speak of a poem's progressions, of emotions if not of actions, of its building. We are thus presuming that a poem has development, a sense of its own temporal structure. When a poem remains innocent of the knowledge of an ordering temporality, the poem and its meaning are problematic.

These problems are notable at the simplest level of relationship. In essays dealing with aspects of aphasia, or language disturbance, Roman Jakobson makes a distinction between the two opposite tropes of metaphor and metonymy. Assuming that language is predicated upon modes of relation, he distinguishes between the internal relation of similarity (and contrast), which underlies metaphor, and the external relation of contiguity (and remoteness), which determines metonymy. Jakobson concludes that any verbal style shows a marked preference for either the metaphoric or metonymic device. Now Dickinson's predilection for the metonymic device is clear. That preference becomes significant when we note that Jakobson's description of a contiguity disorder (the language impairment that affects the perception of context) offers a fairly accurate picture of many of Dickinson's problematic poems. "First," he writes, "the relational words are omitted." Then:

> The syntactical rules organizing words into higher units are lost; this loss, called agrammatism, causes the degeneration of the sentence into a mere "word heap.". . . Word order becomes chaotic; the ties of grammatical coordination and subordination . . . are dissolved. As might be expected, words endowed with purely grammatical functions, like conjunctions, prepositions, pronouns, and articles, disappear first, giving rise to the so-called "telegraphic style."

Jakobson's description resonates against a similar, albeit less technical, comment on Dickinson's poems made by Louis Untermeyer: "The few lines become telegraphic and these telegrams seem not only self-addressed but written in a code." When Jakobson further explains that the type of aphasia affecting contexture tends to give rise to one-sentence utterances and one-word sentences, we recall how many of Dickinson's poems are single sentences. Again, in a less clinical assertion, Donald Thackery writes of Dickinson's "shorthand vocabulary": "One notices how many of her poems seem less concerned with a total conception than with expressing a series of staccato inspirations occurring to her in the form of individual words." In addition, Jakobson asserts that aphasics of this type make frequent use of quasi-metaphors which are based on inexact identification, and his description of that identification is reminiscent of the definitional poems about which I have been speaking. Jakobson concludes: "Since the hierarchy of linguistic units is a superposition of ever larger contexts, the contiguity disorder which affects the construction of contexts destroys this hierarchy." We recall [Dickinson critic Albert] Gelpi's words: "The very confusion of the syntax . . . forces the reader to concentrate on the basic verbal units and derive the strength and meaning largely from the circumference of words."

I have mentioned the Jakobson studies with hesitation, for it would be a mistake to assume that we could diagnose such a disorder from Dickinson's poems. Perhaps the primary reason for citing Jakobson is not to make a brash connection between disease and poetic style, but rather to query the curiosity of relationship between statements so essentially alien: literary criticism of a particular poet, and the description of a linguistic disorder. For one is obliged to note that the predilection for definitional statements, many of which are of a quasi-metaphoric nature, the frequent omission of words that perform grammatical functions, and the absence of contextual clarity bear a striking relationship to Jakobson's description of a contiguity disorder, and that his description brings together and clarifies many of the earlier critical assertions about the poems. Insofar as poetic speech is a violation of the linguistic status quo, it should come as no surprise that such speech deviates from the ordinary configurations that bear our meanings out. That the deviations take these particular forms, however, is a fact that invites interpretation even as it mystifies any summary conclusions.

Dickinson's Tone of Voice Lends Credibility to Difficult Subjects

Archibald MacLeish

Emily Dickinson wrote about death, despair, and God with great skill. As three-time Pulitzer Prize–winning poet and playwright Archibald MacLeish points out, she does so without becoming pretentious or overly sentimental. MacLeish admires the person-to-person nature of her poetry and the restraint that seems the natural voice of a New England woman.

By comparing Dickinson's poems to those of Donne, Rilke, Yeats, and Pound, MacLeish offers evidence of Dickinson's greatness and argues that, in some cases, Dickinson's achievements surpass those of the other poets.

No one can read these poems . . . without perceiving that he is not so much reading as being spoken to. There is a curious energy in the words and a tone like no other most of us have ever heard. Indeed, it is the tone rather than the words that one remembers afterwards. Which is why one comes to a poem of Emily's one has never read before as to an old friend.

But what then is the tone? How does this unforgettable voice speak to us? For one thing, and most obviously, it is a wholly spontaneous tone. There is no literary assumption of posture or pose in advance. There is no sense that a subject has been chosen—that a theme is about to be developed. Occasionally, in the nature pieces, the sunset scenes, which are so numerous in the early poems, one feels the presence of the pad of water-color paper and the mixing of the tints, but when she began to write as poet, which she did, miraculously, within a few months of her beginnings as a writer, all that awkwardness disappears. Breath is drawn and there are words that will not leave you time to watch her coming to-

Archibald MacLeish, "The Private World," in *Emily Dickinson: Three Views* (Amherst, MA: Amherst College Press, 1960). Reprinted by permission of Amherst College Press.

ward you. Poem after poem—more than a hundred and fifty of them—begins with the word "I," the talker's word. She is already in the poem before she begins it, as a child is already in the adventure before he finds a word to speak of it. To put it in other terms, few poets and they among the most valued—Donne comes again to mind—have written more *dramatically* than Emily Dickinson, more in the live locutions of dramatic speech, words born living on the tongue, written as though spoken. It is almost impossible to begin one of her successful poems without finishing it. The punctuation may bewilder you. The density of the thing said may defeat your understanding. But you will read on nevertheless because you will not be able to stop. Something is being *said* to *you* and you have no choice but hear.

And this is a second characteristic of the voice—that it not only speaks but speaks to *you*. We are accustomed in our time—unhappily accustomed, I think—to the poetry of the overheard soliloquy, the poetry written by the poet to himself or to a little group of the likeminded who can be counted on in advance to "understand." Poetry of this kind can create universes when the poet is Rilke but even in Rilke there is something sealed and unventilated about the creation which sooner or later stifles the birds. The subject of poetry is the human experience and its object must therefore be humanity even in a time like ours when humanity seems to prefer to limit its knowledge of the experience of life to the life the advertisers offer it. It is no excuse to a poet that humanity will not listen. It never has listened unless it was made to—and least of all, perhaps, in those two decades of the Civil War and after in which Emily Dickinson wrote.

The materialism and vulgarity of those years were not as flagrant as the materialism and vulgarity in which we live but the indifference was greater. America was immeasurably farther from Paris, and Amherst was incomparably farther from the rest of America, and in and near Amherst there were less than a dozen people to whom Emily felt she could show her poems—and only certain poems at that. But her poems, notwithstanding, were never written to herself. The voice is never a voice over-heard. It is a voice that speaks to us almost a hundred years later with such an urgency, such an immediacy, that most of us are half in love with this girl we call by her first name, and read with scorn Colonel Higginson's description of her as a "plain, shy little person

... without a single good feature." We prefer to remember her own voice describing her eyes—"like the sherry the guest leaves in the glass."

There is nothing more paradoxical in the whole history of poetry, to my way of thinking, than Emily Dickinson's commitment of that live voice to a private box full of pages and snippets tied together with little loops of thread. Other poets have published to the general world poems capable of speaking only to themselves or to one or two beside. Emily locked away in a chest a voice which cries to all of us of our common life and love and death and fear and wonder.

A LACK OF SELF-PITY

Or rather, does *not* cry. For that is a third characteristic of this unforgettable tone: that it does not clamor at us even when its words are the words of passion or of agony. This is a New England voice—it belongs to a woman who "sees New Englandly"—and it has that New England restraint which is really a self-respect which also respects others. There is a poem of Emily's which none of us can read unmoved— which moves me, I confess, so deeply that I cannot always read it. It is a poem which, in another voice, might indeed have cried aloud, but in hers is quiet. I think it is the quietness which moves me most. It begins with these six lines:

> I can wade Grief—
> Whole Pools of it—
> I'm used to that—
> But the least push of Joy
> Breaks up my feet—
> And I tip—drunken

One has only to consider what this might have been, written otherwise by another hand—for it would have had to be another hand. Why is it not maudlin with self-pity here? Why does it truly touch the heart and the more the more it is read? Because it is impersonal? It could scarcely be more personal. Because it is oblique?—Ironic? It is as candid as agony itself. No, because there *IS* no self-pity. Because the tone which can contain "But the least push of Joy/Breaks up my feet" is incapable of self-pity. Emily is not only the actor in this poem, she is the removed observer of the action also. When we drown in self-pity we throw ourselves into ourselves and go down. But the writer of this poem is both in it and out of it: both suffers it and sees. Which is to say that she is poet.

There is another famous poem which makes the same point:

> She bore it till the simple veins
> Traced azure on her hand—
> Till pleading, round her quiet eyes
> The purple Crayons stand.

> Till Daffodils had come and gone
> I cannot tell the sum,
> And then she ceased to bear it
> And with the Saints sat down.

Here again, as so often in her poems of death—and death is, of course, her constant theme—the margin between mawkishness and emotion is thin, so thin that another woman, living, as she lived, in constant contemplation of herself, might easily have stumbled through. But here again what saves her, and saves the poem, is the tone: "She bore it till..." "And then she ceased to bear it/And with the Saints sat down." If you have shaped your mouth to say "And with the Saints sat down" you cannot very well weep for yourself or for anyone else, veins purple on the hand or not.

LETTERS AND POEMS SHARE SIMILAR THEMES

As do her poems, Dickinson's personal letters, including many she wrote to Dr. and Mrs. J.G. Holland, reveal an intimate world that includes insects and birds and a heaven that would be incomplete without neighbors. This excerpt can be found in Letters of Emily Dickinson.

I'd love to be a bird or bee, that whether hum or sing, still might be near. . . .

Heaven is large—is it not? Life is short too, isn't it? Then when one is done, is there not another, and—and—then if God is willing, we are neighbors then.

Anyone who will read Emily's poems straight through in their chronological order in Thomas H. Johnson's magnificent Harvard edition will feel, I think, as I do, that without her extraordinary mastery of tone her achievement would have been impossible. To write constantly of death, of grief, of despair, of agony, of fear is almost to insure the failure of art, for these emotions overwhelm the mind and art must surmount experience to master it. A morbid art is an imperfect art. Poets must learn Yeats's lesson that life is tragedy but if the tragedy turns tragic for them they will be crippled poets. Like the ancient Chinese in *Lapis Lazuli,* like our own beloved Robert Frost who has looked as long and deeply into the darkness of the world as a man well can, "their eyes, their ancient glittering eyes" must be *gay.* Emily's eyes, color of the sherry the guests leave in the glass, had that light in them:

> Dust is the only Secret—
> Death, the only One
> You cannot find out all about
> In his "native town."
>
> Nobody knew "his Father"—
> Never was a Boy—
> Hadn't any playmates,
> Or "Early history"—
>
> Industrious! Laconic!
> Punctual! Sedate!
> Bold as a Brigand!
> Stiller than a Fleet!
>
> Builds, like a Bird, too!
> Christ robs the Nest—
> Robin after Robin
> Smuggled to Rest!

Ezra Pound, in his translation of *The Women of Trachis,* has used a curiously compounded colloquialism which depends on just such locutions to make the long agony of Herakles supportable. Emily had learned the secret almost a century before.

But it is not only agony she is able to put in a supportable light by her mastery of tone. She can do the same thing with those two opposing subjects which betray so many poets: herself and God. She sees herself as small and lost and doubtless doomed—but she sees herself always, or almost always, with a saving smile which is not entirely tender:

> Two full Autumns for the Squirrel
> Bounteous prepared—
> Nature, Hads't thou not a Berry
> For thy wandering Bird?

and

> I was a Phebe—nothing more—
> A Phebe—nothing less—
> The little note that others dropt
> I fitted into place—
>
> I dwelt too low that any seek—
> Too shy, that any blame—

> A Phebe makes a little print
> Upon the Floors of Fame—

and

> A Drunkard cannot meet a Cork
> Without a Revery—
> And so encountering a Fly
> This January Day
> Jamaicas of Remembrance stir
> That send me reeling in—
> The moderate drinker of Delight
> Does not deserve the spring—

I suppose there was never a more delicate dancing on the crumbling edge of the abyss of self-pity—that suicidal temptation of the lonely—than Emily's, but she rarely tumbles in. She sees herself in the awkward stumbling attitude and laughs.

THE SUBJECT OF GOD

As she laughs too, but with a child's air of innocence, at her father's Puritan God, that Neighbor over the fence of the next life in the hymnal:

> Abraham to kill him
> Was distinctly told—
> Isaac was an Urchin—
> Abraham was old—
>
> Not a hesitation—
> Abraham complied—
> Flattered by Obeisance
> Tyranny demurred—
>
> Isaac—to his children
> Lived to tell the tale—
> Moral—with a Mastiff
> Manners may prevail.

It is a little mocking sermon which would undoubtedly have shocked Edward Dickinson with his "pure and terrible" heart, but it brings the god of Abraham closer to New England than he had been for the two centuries preceding— brings him, indeed, as close as the roaring lion in the yard: so close that he can be addressed politely by that child who always walked with Emily hand in hand:

> Lightly stepped a yellow star
> To its lofty place
> Loosed the Moon her silver hat
> From her lustral Face
> All of the Evening softly lit

As an Astral Hall
Father I observed to Heaven
You are punctual—

But more important than the confiding smile which makes it possible to speak familiarly to the God of Elder Brewster is the hot and fearless and wholly human anger with which she is able to face him at the end. Other poets have confronted God in anger but few have been able to manage it without rhetoric and posture. There is something about that ultimate face to face which excites and embarrassing self-consciousness in which the smaller of the two opponents seems to strut and "beat it out even to the edge of doom." Not so with Emily. She speaks with the laconic restraint appropriate to her country, which is New England, and herself, which is a small, shy gentlewoman who has suffered much:

Of God we ask one favor,
That we may be forgiven—
For what, he is presumed to know—
The Crime, from us, is hidden—
Immured the whole of Life
Within a magic Prison

It is a remarkable poem and its power, indeed its possibility, lies almost altogether in its voice, its tone. The figure of the magic prison is beautiful in itself, but it is effective in the poem because of the level at which the poem is spoken—the level established by that "he is presumed to know." At another level even the magic prison might well become pretentious.

But it is not my contention here that Emily Dickinson's mastery of tone is merely a negative accomplishment, a kind of lime which prepares the loam for clover. On the contrary I should like to submit that her tone is the root itself of her greatness. The source of poetry, as Emily knew more positively than most, is a particular awareness of the world. "It is that," she says, meaning by "that" a poet, which "Distills amazing sense / From ordinary Meanings," and the distillation is accomplished not by necromancy but by perception—by the particularity of the perception—which makes what is "ordinary meaning" to the ordinary, "amazing sense" to the poet. The key to the poetry of any poem, therefore, is its particularity—the uniqueness of its vision of the world it sees. In some poems the particularity can be found in the images into which the vision is translated. In others it seems to exist in the rhythm which carries the vision "alive into the heart."

In still others it is found in a play of mind which breaks the light of the perception like a prism. The particularity has as many forms almost as there are poets capable of the loneliness in which uniqueness is obliged to live. With Emily Dickinson it is the tone and timbre of the speaking voice. When she first wrote Colonel Higginson to send him copies of her verses she asked him to tell her if they "breathed" and the word, like all her words, was deliberately chosen. She knew, I think, what her verses were, for she knew everything that concerned her.

I should like to test my case, if I can call it that, on a short poem of four lines written probably on the third anniversary of her father's death. It is one of her greatest poems and perhaps the only poem she ever wrote which carries the curious and solemn weight of perfection. I should like you to consider wherein this perfection lies:

Lay this Laurel on the One
Too intrinsic for Renown—
Laurel—vail your deathless tree—
Him you chasten, that is He!

Play as a Theme in Dickinson's Poems

Anand Rao Thota

A native of India, Anand Rao Thota became especially interested in Emily Dickinson after hearing Archibald MacLeish deliver a lecture on the poet at Harvard. In his book *Emily Dickinson's Poetry*, Thota makes comparisons between Dickinson's work and Indian classics such as *Rig Veda*.

Though, as Thota says in his preface to his book, he has "read all other critical studies or biographies" of Dickinson, he tries to keep his arguments free from their influence and to discuss his findings in clear, everyday language.

In this essay, previously published in *Dickinson Studies*, a scholarly journal limited to the study of Emily Dickinson, Thota notices how often the subject of play is raised in her work.

One of the recurring words in Emily Dickinson's poems and letters is "play," which has critical significance. Poetry, as she affirms to Higginson, was her only "playmate": "you asked me if I wrote now? I have no other playmate—."

Dickinson records in a playful tone scenes from nature which were a constant source of ecstasy for her:

The Bird did prance—the Bee did play—
The Sun ran miles away

One of the most amusing compositions of Dickinson is on the play of seasons around a mountain. The ideas and experiences are orchestrated through words that literally portray a scene of "play" in nature:

The Mountain sat upon the Plain

Dickinson is unique in describing the play of seasons with such an enchantment that she equates the experience with that of a contact with "Eternity":

Indifferent Seasons doubtless play

Anand Rao Thota, "Play in Dickinson," *Dickinson Studies*, no. 46, bonus issue, 1983.

PLAY AND NATURE

Even fearful scenes of nature have their moments of play—Dickinsonian version of DISCORDIA CONCORS, a technique which is very remote to the romantic mode and akin to that of the metaphysicals. She succeeds through her poetry in projecting a playful mood in spite of the fact she describes an awful scene.

The Clouds their Backs together laid

This playful attitude that Dickinson succeeds in projecting through her poems is very significant because the subject described in a few poems is relegated to the background and quite another message is conveyed. For instance, the following lines of the poem are palpably a description of "The Lightning"; but, ultimately, they project the puritan conception of God.

The Lightning playeth—all the while—

PLAY AS A STRATEGY

This complex use of the word play by Dickinson is neither casual nor accidental. In fact, it is a deliberate strategy evolved to withdraw from experience in order to portray it objectively. This is what makes Dickinson's poetry typically unromantic. The personality that is revealed is that of a poet who could write to her cousins just before her death a two-word message "Called Back." She not only distanced herself from her experiences throughout her life but also there is factual evidence through this letter that she could withdraw herself from the experience of her own impending death, and make a playful comment upon it.

Quite early in her career as a poet, Dickinson cultivated her sensibility which is replete with playful stances: "Blessed are they that play, for theirs is the Kingdom of Heaven." It is a remarkable way of coming to terms with life and perhaps a "cunning" strategy to convert its experience into art, echoing, as it does, the Bible: "cunning in playing" (I Samuel 16:18). Dickinson acknowledges this aspect of her life and art when she writes . . .

It is easy to work when the soul is at play—

When the experiences in life tease her "Like a Panther in the Glove," she counters the situation by adopting a pose of play.

I play at Riches—to appease

Dickinson applies the strategy of play to reveal complex implications that her poems embody. She refers to the confrontation between God and Moses in the poem 597. The Biblical episode is introduced by playing with the idea of Moses himself, who is called "Old Moses." While dealing with the incident of the Bible, she plays down the Bible itself: "And tho' in soberer moments—/No Moses there can be/I'm satisfied—." Because, to her, it is just a "Romance." But further still in the poem the historical event of the meeting between God and Moses is stated as "tantalizing play" between two boys, tho' not of equal strength:

While God's adroiter will

On Moses—seemed to fasten
With tantalizing Play
As Boy—should deal with lesser Boy—
To prove ability.

The stark reality of "tomb" is also not outside her playful poetic grasp even in the later phase of her poetic career:

Sweet hours have perished here;
   This is a mighty room;
Within its precincts hopes have played,—
   Now shadows in the tomb.

PLAY AND MEMORY

There are scores of poems by Dickinson which center around the idea of play. The source of this play is recollection: "When Memory rings her Bell, let all Thoughts run in." Recollection does not, as in Wordsworth, flash on the "inward eye" and result, as it were, in a mystic stance: "bliss of the solitude." In Dickinson, recollection "plays" and re-enacts the life experiences with all their sound and fury, signifying not only the past experiences but also that are in store after this earthly existence.

Over and over, like a Tune—

While describing the play of recollection, Dickinson indulges in striking psychological speculation annihilating the concepts of time—of past, of present and of future. The play of recollection unites the past with the present and also anticipates the future in the present, by affording an imaginative glimpse through "Cornets of Paradise." Thus "Phantom Battlements" become the melting pot for the three aspects of time.

Studying the conditions of her life with "a Hum," Dickinson strives to present playfully her experiences through her poems that reveal all the liveliness of the situation that is being poetically worked out. She makes the process significant through a playful scrutiny of the issues that confronted her times. Dickinson was conditioned, esthetically speaking, to develop a counter-point to puritan culture which engulfed her socially. Deprived of the avenues for revolt against a superficially monolithic but internally disintegrating culture, which frowned on deviation, she withdrew herself from the culture to rise above it to record her amused observations in her letters and poems.

Dickinson's Style Broke with Convention

Cheryl Walker

While other women were publishing long, flowery reflections on love, faith, and beauty, Dickinson's poems fit the writer's complex ideas into short, tight sentences, with a vocabulary hardly considered appropriate to the feminine sensibility of her time. Aware of public expectations, Dickinson continued to write about "feminine" subjects such as unattainable love, but in a complex manner that called certain conventions into question.

In the following excerpt, scholar Cheryl Walker uses four passages by Dickinson to illustrate the genius of a woman she compares to a more compressed, more obscure Shakespeare. Walker is the author of *The Nightingale's Burden: Women Poets and American Culture Before 1900*.

[What] distinguishes Emily Dickinson from other women poets is her skill with words, her use of language. She retained her compression despite pressure from her closest friends and critics, people like Samuel Bowles and T.W. Higginson, who would have made her more discursive. She introduced unusual vocabulary into women's poetry—vocabulary borrowed from various professions mainly closed to women, like law, medicine, the military, and merchandising. I agree with critic Adrienne Rich that she knew she was a genius. Nothing else could explain her peculiar invulnerability to contemporary criticism of her work.

Dickinson wrote many poems about violation. The integrity of some poems was literally violated by editors who made unauthorized changes before printing them. But the poet triumphed in the end. She created a unique voice in American poetry and would not modulate it, even for Higginson who directed her to writers like Maria Lowell and Helen Hunt Jackson as models.

Like Lowell and Jackson, Dickinson did not look down on the female poetic subjects of her day. She used them; but she used them in what would come to be perceived as a poetic assault on the feminine conventions from which they sprung. She was not, for instance, taken in by the propaganda of "true womanhood." She saw behind the virtue of modesty the caricature of the double-bind.

> A Charm invests a face
> Imperfectly beheld—
> The Lady dare not lift her Vail
> For fear it be dispelled—
>
> But peers beyond her mesh—
> And wishes—and denies—
> Lest Interview—annul a want
> That Image—satisfies—

Perhaps Dickinson's ambivalent relation to the world has more to do with this lady "who dare not lift her Vail" than has previously been perceived. What this poem captures is the feelings of a woman who must obtain what she wants through deception and manipulation. Thus it does not simply represent the familiar Dickinson wisdom that hunger tantalizes where satiety cloys. This woman's feelings become part of the substance of the poem. They are fear (of male rejection), curiosity, and desire. The lady must finally deny her desires, sublimate her will to power, and assume a passive role. "A Charm" might also serve as a commentary on a poem written three years earlier.

> Our lives are Swiss—
> So still—so Cool—
> Till some odd afternoon
> The Alps neglect their Curtains
> And we look farther on!
>
> *Italy* stands the other side!
> While like a guard between—
> The solemn Alps—
> The siren Alps
> Forever intervene!

We recognize the theme of the unattained. . . . Here, however, the barriers both forbid assault and invite it. They are both awesome and enticing. Like the lady who "peers beyond her mesh," this speaker hasn't accepted the limitations on her experience. Though undemonstrative, she remains unreconciled.

The insights made available by the comparison of these two poems can help us even when we examine the particular language that made Dickinson unique. Take, for example, the following poem written during her most creative period.

I had not minded—Walls—
Were Universe—one Rock—
And far I heard his silver Call
The other side the Block—

I'd tunnel—till my Groove
Pushed sudden thro' to his—
Then my face take her Recompense—
The looking in his Eyes—

But 'tis a single Hair—
A filament—a law—
A Cobweb—wove in Adamant—
A Battlement—of Straw—

A limit like the Vail
Unto the Lady's face—
But every Mesh—a Citadel—
And Dragons—in the Crease—

This is a poem about the forbidden lover, and as such it reminds us of what Dickinson could do with conventional female subjects. Although this is not one of Dickinson's best poems, it exhibits many of her characteristic innovations and therefore makes an interesting focus for discussion. Does this poem have roots in real experience or was it merely an exercise?

In [a] letter, probably composed about this time and intended for a recipient we can no longer identify, the poet asked: "Couldn't Carlo [her dog], and you and I walk in the meadows an hour—and nobody care but the Bobolink—and *his*—a *silver* scruple? I used to think when I died—I could see you—so I died as fast as I could—but the 'Corporation' are going Heaven too so [Eternity] wont be sequestered—now [at all]—". Here we find the familiar impossible attachment forbidden by "the Corporation," the constituted powers. It is an attachment that can only be indulged in secret, in some "sequestered" place. This letter has too much unrefined feeling in it to be the product of a merely literary pose, and I suggest that the poem was also written out of felt experience, although the structural properties this experience assumed may well have been influenced by the vocabulary of secret sorrow.

Dickinson begins "I had not minded—Walls" in the subjunctive, one of her characteristic modes. Thus, she establishes the initial grounds of the poem as those of the nonreal, the if. The first two stanzas posit a set of circumstances that would allow for fulfillment, the enticement of the view. . . . The last two stanzas, in contrast, describe the limitations on fulfillment that forever intervene. . . .

Although the words themselves do not always mean what their sounds convey ("citadel" being used to suggest an obstacle instead of a possibility), there is at the levels of both meaning and sound a sense of opposition: desire vs. frustration. Dickinson's language operates on the basis of paired antitheses. Other pairings include the concrete vs. the abstract (face/recompense) the material vs. the immaterial (rock/silver call), and the hard vs. the soft (adamant/cobweb). Her code is conflict.

Thus far we might compare her use of language to Shakespeare's, which also depends upon doublings, paradoxes, contrasts. However, Dickinson, though she loved Shakespeare, chose to be more obscure, and she did this largely by breaking linguistic rules out of a commitment to compression. The first stanza, for instance, might be paraphrased: I would not have minded walls. Were the universe to have been entirely made up of rock and were I to have heard his call from afar, it would have seemed to me merely a short distance, the other side of the block. This, of course, reduces the impact of Dickinson's compression. "Block" in her poem affects one like a pun, reminding us of "rock" earlier, as well as of the geographical meaning of "block," a city street division.

Dickinson was criticized in her day for this kind of compression. It flew in the face of most contemporary poetry, which aimed at comprehensiveness through discursive exposition. Emerson was probably her closest friend here, but even he did not break rules as flagrantly as she. Her editors also grumbled at her rhymes. "His" and "eyes" did not seem like rhyming words to them. . . .

Furthermore, in the sequence filament/law, cobweb/adamant, and battlement/straw there is a reversal of terms in the final pair. The first two move from the insubstantial to the substantive, the last one from the substantive back to the insubstantial. "Adamant" is echoed in "battlement," but the "law" becomes "straw."

The structural progression from the real to the surreal is

recognizably characteristic of Dickinson. And here the lines, "A limit like the Vail / Unto the Lady's face," become significant. Like the veil, the limitations Dickinson describes are restrictive in the real world. The seemingly insubstantial "hair" is tougher than rock, and like the veil of restrictions women must accept, to pass beyond these limitations forces one to encounter terrible dragons. However, a citadel, the *Oxford English Dictionary* tells us, is a "fortress commanding a city, which it serves both to protect and to keep in subjugation." Like the prison, this image reminds us of Dickinson's Houdini-like ability to wriggle out of confining spaces, to convert limitations into creative resources. Dragons are at least interesting to contemplate. The lady's veil—the symbol of Dickinson's sense of social, legal, and literary restrictions—provided her with a certain recompense. Thus the reversal in the third stanza, where limiting law becomes insubstantial straw, works.

Ultimately, Emily Dickinson transformed her closed world into a creative space. If there is a disappointment in this poem, it comes in the second stanza where "the looking in his eyes" seems a rather weak way of describing this triumph. But whatever its limitations, this poem shows us the way an artist like Dickinson could make interesting use of motifs such as the secret sorrow and the forbidden lover. Her vision was "slant," and therefore to us thoroughly refreshing.

WORK SURPASSES TRADITIONAL EXPECTATIONS

Recently it has become fashionable to see Emily Dickinson as a woman who lived in the realm of transcendence, secure in the space she created for the exercise of her power. Although I am sympathetic with this view, I would like to add a word of caution. No one can read Dickinson's poems and letters in their entirety without a sense that the ground for security was forever shifting under her feet. She did not resort to references to fear only out of coyness. She felt it. She wrote: "In all the circumference of Expression, those guileless words of Adam and Eve never were surpassed, 'I was afraid and hid Myself.'" And elsewhere: "Your bond to your brother reminds me of mine to my sister—early, earnest, indissoluble. Without her life were fear, and Paradise a cowardice, except for her inciting voice." To rejoice that she found ways of evading the subjugation of the spirit that her society enforced upon its women should not mean ignoring her sense of vulnerability, which was real, which was tragic. In Dickinson's preoccupation with the imagery of royalty, we find her desire to exercise the full range of her talents; we find her will to power. In her preoccupation with falling, surrendering, confinement, and violation, we find her fears. Knowing what she had to give up, recognition within her lifetime, the chance to remain within the world she devoured information about through her friends and her newspaper, we can only be glad that at moments she had the perspective to write:

> The Heart is the Capital of the Mind—
> The Mind is a single State—
> The Heart and the Mind together make
> A single Continent—
>
> One is the Population—
> Numerous enough—
> This ecstatic Nation
> Seek—it is Yourself.

The puzzle of Emily Dickinson's work is finally not a question of the identity of [her mysterious love interest] or the extent of her real experience, but one of tradition and the individual talent. Although the concern with intense feeling, the ambivalence toward power, the fascination with death, the forbidden lover and secret sorrow all belong to this women's tradition, Emily Dickinson's best work so far surpasses anything that a logical extension of that tradition's codes could have produced that the only way to explain it is by the single word, genius. She was "of the Druid." That a great many poems like "I tie my Hat—I crease my Shawl" are in places not much above the women's poetry of her time is only to be expected. What Emily Dickinson did for later women poets, like Amy Lowell who wanted to write her biography, was remarkable: she gave them dignity. No other aspect of her influence was so important. After Emily Dickinson's work became known, women poets in America could take their work seriously. She redeemed the poetess for them, and made her a genuine poet.

CHRONOLOGY

1830

Emily Elizabeth Dickinson born December 10 in Amherst, Massachusetts.

1833

Sister Lavinia (Vinnie) born.

1842

Emily's father, Edward Dickinson, is elected state senator of Massachusetts.

1844

Religious revival in Amherst.

1845

Mexican-American War begins; Texas admitted to the Union.

1847

Emily attends Mount Holyoke Seminary for Girls.

1848

Seneca Falls Declaration marks beginning of women's rights movement.

1850

Edward Dickinson, Vinnie Dickinson, and Susan Gilbert join First Church of Christ during revival meeting in Amherst.

1852

Springfield Republican publishes Emily's valentine.

1853

Austin Dickinson, Emily's brother, enters Harvard Law School, becomes engaged to Susan.

1855

Edward and Austin become law partners.

1856

Austin joins First Church of Christ, marries Susan Gilbert; Austin and Susan move into the Evergreens, built by Edward Dickinson next door to the Homestead; Mrs. Dickinson's long illness begins.

1857

Emerson lectures in Amherst, stays with Austin and Sue.

1858

Orphaned cousins Clara and Anna Newman arrive as wards of Edward Dickinson, live with Austin and Susan at the Evergreens.

1859

Darwin's *Origin of the Species* is published.

1861

Civil War begins; first child, Edward (Ned), born to Austin and Sue; *Springfield Republican* publishes "I Taste a Liquor never brewed—"; "Evolution vs. Creationism" debated by Thomas Henry Huxley and Bishop Samuel Wilberforce.

1862

Springfield Republican publishes "Safe in their Alabaster Chambers"; Emily responds to letter asking for contributors to the *Atlantic Monthly*, beginning her correspondence with Colonel Thomas Higginson.

1863

Lincoln issues Emancipation Proclamation.

1864

Two more poems of Dickinson's printed; Emily in Boston for seven months for medical treatment for her eyes.

1865

General Lee surrenders; Lincoln assassinated.

1866

Daughter, Martha, born to Austin and Susan.

1869

Transcontinental railroad joined at Promontory Point, Utah.

1870

Emily receives visit by Thomas Wentworth Higginson.

1873

Austin elected treasurer of Amherst College.

1874

Edward Dickinson dies.

1875

Mrs. Dickinson becomes bedridden due to a stroke.

1880

Austin has first bout with malaria.

1881

President Garfield shot.

1882

Austin begins affair with Mabel Loomis Todd; Mabel sings for Emily behind a closed door; mother Emily Norcross Dickinson dies.

1883

Nephew Gilbert Dickinson dies.

1884

Emily has first attack of kidney disease.

1886

Emily Dickinson dies.

1890

Poems published, edited by Thomas Higginson and Mabel Loomis Todd.

1891

Second series of *Poems* published, edited by Todd and Higginson.

1894

Letters of Emily Dickinson published, edited by Mabel Loomis Todd.

1895

Austin dies.

1896

Third series of *Poems* published, edited by Todd; Vinnie successfully sues Todd for copyright ownership.

1899

Vinnie dies.

1913

Susan dies.

1914

The Single Hound published, edited by Martha Dickinson Bianchi.

FOR FURTHER RESEARCH

Millicent Todd Bingham, *Ancestors' Brocades: The Literary Debut of Emily Dickinson*. New York: Harper & Brothers, 1945.

Caesar R. Blake and Carlton F. Wells, *The Recognition of Emily Dickinson: Selected Criticism Since 1890*. Ann Arbor: University of Michigan Press, 1965.

Harold Bloom, ed., *Emily Dickinson*. New York: Chelsea House, 1985.

Carl Bode, ed., *Midcentury America: Life in the 1850s*. Carbondale and Edwardsville: Southern Illinois University Press, 1972.

Joanne Dobson, *Dickinson and the Strategies of Reticence: The Woman Writer in Nineteenth-Century America*. Bloomington: Indiana University Press, 1989.

Paul Ferlazzo, ed., *Critical Essays on Emily Dickinson*. Boston: G.K. Hall, 1984.

Albert J. Gelpi, *Emily Dickinson: The Mind of a Poet*. Cambridge, MA: Harvard University Press, 1966.

Daniel Walker Howe, ed., *Victorian America*. Philadelphia: University of Pennsylvania Press, 1976.

Suzanne Juhasz, ed., *Feminist Critics Read Emily Dickinson*. Bloomington: Indiana University Press, 1983.

Richard H. Rupp, *Critics on Emily Dickinson*. Coral Gables: University of Miami Press, 1972.

Richard B. Sewall, *The Life of Emily Dickinson*. New York: Farrar, Straus and Giroux, 1974.

William R. Sherwood, *Circumference and Circumstance: Stages in the Mind and Art of Emily Dickinson*. New York: Columbia University Press, 1968.

Judy Jo Small, *Positive as Sound: Emily Dickinson's Rhyme.* Athens: University of Georgia Press, 1990.

Barton Levi St. Armand, *Emily Dickinson and Her Culture: The Soul's Society.* Cambridge, England: Cambridge University Press, 1984.

U.S. Civil War Centennial Commission, *The United States on the Eve of the Civil War: As Described in the 1860 Census.* Washington, D.C.: U.S. Government Printing Office, 1963.

Cynthia Griffin Wolf, *Emily Dickinson.* New York: Knopf, 1986.

WORKS BY EMILY DICKINSON

Poems by Emily Dickinson (1890)
Poems by Emily Dickinson, Second Series (1891)
Letters of Emily Dickinson, 2 vols. (1894)
Poems by Emily Dickinson, Third Series (1896)
The Single Hound (1914)
Further Poems of Emily Dickinson (1929)
Unpublished Poems of Emily Dickinson (1935)
Bolts of Melody (1945)
The Poems of Emily Dickinson, 3 vols. (1955)
The Complete Poems of Emily Dickinson (1960)

INDEX